FOUND

Dedicated To
Beloved Gurus & Startup Mentors

FOUND

Transforming Your Unlimited Ideas Into One Sustainable Business

NAVEEN LAKKUR
WITH DR. LIZ ALEXANDER

FOREWORD BY ADEO RESSI,
FOUNDER & CEO, THE FOUNDER INSTITUTE

INDIA • SINGAPORE • MALAYSIA

FOUND: Transforming Your Unlimited Ideas into One Sustainable Business

Copyright © Naveen Lakkur

First Published in India in 2016 by Lone Tree Books

Republished by Notion press

All Rights Reserved.

ISBN 979-8-88986-951-1

Illustrations design by Priya Kumar, New Delhi

The stock photography comes from: Fotolia: https://us.fotolia.com
© designsstock - Fotolia.com and © indigolotos - Fotolia.com

Disclaimer

This book expresses the views of the authors and any depiction herein may have real association or connection intended or should be inferred with the author as these examples serve as sources to support a standpoint. Various illustrations and anecdotes are captured from numerous sources, which for reasons beyond control, couldn't be explicitly quoted. Hence, the author makes no claim, explicit or implicit, about the ownership of any such occurrence in this document about any instance or incident.

The contents in this book are subject to change or, may change without notice.

All brand names, product names, figures, referrals, trademarks, registered trademarks or trade names used in this book are property of their respective holders/owners. Authors & Publisher is not associated with any product or vendor mentioned in this book.

Advance Praise for FOUND

"Innovations are the engine of economic growth in the world. This book truly inspires future entrepreneurs to realize what it takes to contribute to that growth by transforming their ideas into viable businesses. FOUND is a "must-have" resource, providing the insight that aspiring entrepreneurs need to become accomplished businesspeople. Anyone committed to enhancing their creativity and thoughtfulness in order to build that one sustainable, entrepreneurial venture will find immense value in this wonderful book."

Karan Kumar H, Serial Entrepreneur and Mentor to Start-up Ventures

"At a time when burning investor cash is increasingly fashionable and the venture itself is often the product on sale for many an entrepreneur seeking quick money from the start-up boom, FOUND asks the right question: Are you ready to give the next 20 years of your life to this idea to see it working? That is at the heart of the current dilemma faced by entrepreneurs: finding the right idea that so fires you up that you are willing to bet a lifetime on it. This book is a must-read for entrepreneurs *not* in the business of churning out companies for sale. When the dust settles after the current euphoria, it will be entrepreneurs of this variety who can look back and say I created something that has lasting value."

Denny Kurien, President & CEO, Keiretsu Forum, Bangalore

FOUND

"Successful businesses have emerged from finding simple solutions to the burning problems around us. FOUND is filled with good insights, upbeat stories and solid suggestions. In this book Naveen, in a very simple style, talks about the harsh realities of most aspiring entrepreneurs who fail to realize that every good idea doesn't necessarily have the potential to become a viable business. The steps you need to take in order to arrive at a single executable idea that could support and grow your business are relevant and refreshing. This is a must read."

Geetha Ramamurthy, Co-Founder and CEO, Career Confidence and Advisor, Keiretsu, International Angel Investor Forum

"Everybody has ideas, what matters is what we do with them. At some point you may have thought to yourself: 'I had an idea like that some time ago and now another person has turned it into a commercial reality!' Don't risk that happening to you again. Read FOUND and practice the exercises contained in its page so you can identify, nurture and actually do something about the ideas you have. Use this excellent blueprint for success to stay on top and execute in the right way."

Rajesh Kannan, Co-founder & CEO, Compassites Software Solutions

Leaders and entrepreneurs are continuously searching for ways and models to become more effective and relevant. FOUND is another masterpiece from Naveen Lakkur. It touches on how to drive ongoing sustainable success by creating an environment of cultivating, capturing and maximizing the unlimited ideas that enable organizations to scale up and speed up their goals. This quality book is rich in actionable insights and practical advice towards achieving inspired organizational transformation. Definitely an essential read !

Sanjay Rughani, CEO, Standard Chartered Bank Tanzania Limited and Member, IFAC Professional Accountants in Business Committee (PAIBC)

"Discipline is the wire frame around which you build your business. It helps you counter the hurdles which one invariably comes across in the journey of entrepreneurship. VCs are not always impressed by unbridled creativity alone—they like to see it being channelled effectively, in a systematic manner. FOUND gives you the architecture and the discipline to ensure success in your startup by choosing the right idea."

Srikanth Bhagavat, Founder & Principal Advisor, Hexagon Wealth

About the Authors

NAVEEN LAKKUR

Naveen Lakkur is a serial entrepreneur turned Innovation Coach. Naveen loves to inspire enterprises & entrepreneurs to innovate and guide them to grow in the right direction.

In his professional career spanning 25+ years in the industry worldwide, he has co-founded several innovative companies. He has also been a catalyst for 250+ ideas to have become commercial realities. Naveen Lakkur is the Founder & Chief Innovation Coach at the Institute of Inspiring Innovation. He is passionate about sharing his practical knowledge of building companies and nurturing ideas. He brings to the table his personal experience of a unique combination of 'Systemic Innovation ~ A Structured and Scalable Approach' and 'Tactical Innovation ~ A Frugal and Flexible Approach. Besides his active engagement with the industry, he indulges in writing books with international recognitions and he loves telling business stories.

Visit **www.NaveenLakkur.com** to know more.

Dr. LIZ ALEXANDER

Liz Alexander, Ph.D., has been an ideator since 1984, when her first book was published in the U.K. Since then she has nurtured her own creativity and that of her clients by authoring or co-authoring 15 more internationally published nonfiction books, many of which are best-sellers and have attracted multiple international awards. She sums up her portfolio career in one word: Communicator.

Liz considers herself a global citizen. Born in Scotland, she was raised in England and moved to the U.S. in 2009. She currently lives in Austin, Texas, visits India on business several times a year, and her co-founder of boutique consultancy, Leading Thought (**www.leadingthought.us.com**) is based in Sydney, Australia.

She acts as book strategist and consulting co-author to senior executives and entrepreneurs worldwide (**www.drlizalexander.com**), and is Special Counsel, Book Strategist & Writer for SenateSHJ, Australasia's largest privately-owned PR firm.

Most recently, Liz's contribution to innovative thinking has been recognized by the international research institute on thought leadership, The Dutch School of Thought in Eindhoven, Holland.

(http://dutchschoolofthought.com/liz-alexander/)

Dr. Alexander's gift and talent lies in guiding clients to communicate in ways that intrigue, influence and positively impact their target market, leading to business growth and sustainability. As an educator with three degrees in educational psychology, she developed and taught the Strategic Communication Certificate Program for The University of Texas at Austin's Professional Development Center.

Acknowledgments

I t would take a whole a book to list all the names and the roles that people have played, directly or indirectly, in this journey of mine from idea generation to my current stage of "catalyst for ideation." So let me simply begin these acknowledgments by thanking all the aspiring entrepreneurs I have met over the years who have helped to inspire me, not least in even considering writing down my thoughts. It is because of these courageous individuals who sought my mentorship and went on to transform their ideas into meaningful companies that I feel sure this book will significantly increase the success rate of startups.

I wish to recognize the efforts of all my mentors: V.V.Ranganathan, Murali Vullaganti, Jnan Dash, R.V.S. Rao, A.V. Bhaskar, Kannan Ayyar, A.N.Rao, Gopal Rao, and William & Debra Miller who have helped shape many of my ideas, both intrapreneurial and entrepreneurial, into commercial realities. Some people I have especially learned from, such as Rob Ryan whose 'Sunflower Model' appears in his book *Smartups*, and Rajesh Setty, a wonderful friend who continually teaches me new concepts and has exposed me to innovative models, structures and approaches for the last two decades. The learning I have gained from them all has transformed itself gradually into the acquired knowledge found in this book.

My association with the Founder Institute has provided me with untold opportunities to associate with many aspiring entrepreneurs and mentors who are passionate in their quest to create meaningful and enduring companies. This has offered me many phenomenal experiences and considerable exposure, so it is with deep gratitude and respect that I acknowledge the staff of Founder Institute, Fellow Directors and Mentors around the world.

It is hard to put into words my heartfelt thanks to all those amazing people who have participated in bringing this book to reality, in addition to their efforts generally in making the intrapreneurial and entrepreneurial journey worthwhile for so many. Thank you to Adeo Ressi for providing the Foreword, as well as the following friends and colleagues who so willingly shared their stories and experiences: Abdul Sait, Ajay Goel, Dayal Nathan, Harry Scrope, Ivan J Goldberg, Janardan Prasad, Mukesh Jha, Poornima Shenoy, Rajeev Pathak, Ram Ramanathan, Ravikiran Annaswamy, Srikanth Acharaya, Srinivas Varadarajan. Thanks also to Denny Kurian, Geetha Ramamurthy, Karan Kumar, Rahul Patwardhan, Rajesh Kannan, Rajesh Setty, Shanti Mohan, Srikanth Bhagavat and Sri Krishna for their advance praise for this book. Each one of them has provided a huge amount of value and I am grateful for their time and generosity of spirit.

A special thanks to my good friend and fellow "Cerebrator," Dr. Liz Alexander for her skill in developing my original concept into this book we call FOUND. Not least, in provoking me to new and deeper thought. Through her questioning process and guidance she has surely transformed this book into one of true thought leadership.

I wish also to thank Priya Kumar for her fantastic efforts in capturing the essence and the intent of the book, which she translated into the wonderful illustrations you will find within these pages. Appreciation goes also to Adina Cucicov of Flamingo Designs, whose great efforts created the cover page and interior layout.

This section is incomplete without acknowledging my mother, my wife Gowri, my son Sriniket and my daughter Srinutaa, together with all the other family members and awesome colleagues and friends who have put up with my ideas and the craziness.

Ultimately, I have God to thank for creating this amazing world and for choosing us to produce this work. Liz and I sincerely hope that the

FOUND process will make a meaningful difference to the success of every intrapreneur & entrepreneur—current and future, experienced and aspiring—who reads this book.

Thank you God!

Naveen Lakkur
Bangalore, India

Contents

Foreword

by Adeo Ressi, the Founder Institute

According to a 2010 study by the Ewing Marion Kauffman Foundation, startups are responsible for all net job creation in the U.S. economy[1].

At the same time, the failure rate for startups is incredibly high. Using a combination of data from the Founder Institute and **TheFunded.com**, in addition to my personal experience working with startups across six continents, I would estimate that of the approximately 25,000 new technology companies started each year around the world, nearly half will fail within the first few months. Of the companies that last more than a few months, less than 100 in a year will grow to have a truly global impact (about .4%).

---

1 Ewing Marion Kauffman Foundation, The importance of Startups in Job Creation and Job Destruction, http://bit.ly/1OO77Ew (accessed December 6, 2015)

Think about that: **Only about four out of every 1,000 startups created each year create a global impact.**

As a lifetime entrepreneur, this to me is a problem of giant proportions. I believe that startups are the global economic engine that create jobs for society, and develop innovations that make the human condition better. How can we push our society forward as quickly as possible when only four out of every 1,000 startups created each year are making a global impact?

There is good news, however.

First, the pool of new companies each year continues to grow as local markets develop, new technologies mature, business funding becomes more prevalent, and the international business world becomes "flatter". If you can grow the pool of companies, you can increase the competition and spawn more innovation and more impact.

Second, and most importantly, a large proportion of startup failure is completely avoidable.

As I mentioned above, almost half of companies fail within the first few months, because most entrepreneurial mistakes are made at the very beginning of the startup process. All the decisions a founder makes in the early stages can be deadly. For example, is the market you are pursuing big enough to sustain a business? Will anybody want the product that you plan to build—and want it enough to pay for it? Are there realistic distribution channels for your product? Do you even have the team to execute on your vision? If you can't answer yes to these questions early on, then you are dead in the water before you even begin.

In my opinion, the potential for economic impact and new job creation is left largely unfulfilled because many aspiring entrepreneurs don't go through a structured process of research, evaluation, and self-assessment before starting their companies. At the nexus of this problem is properly evaluating your startup idea, and this was the inspiration for my starting the Founder Institute.

If there is one thing I know to be true, it is this: a good idea doesn't necessarily make a good business.

In this book, Naveen Lakkur teaches you a structured process to evaluate and iterate on your business ideas, in order to increase your chances of survival and reduce your chances of making deadly mistakes early on.

By following a structured process of research, evaluation, and self-assessment, not only can you increase your chances of survival, you may also save several years of your life and possibly your life savings, by *not starting* an unsustainable company.

I wish you the best of luck on your entrepreneurial endeavors!

Adeo Ressi
San Francisco, USA

BIO:
Adeo Ressi is the Founder & CEO of the Founder Institute (**http://fi.co**), an entrepreneur training and startup launch program that has helped start over 1500 technology companies across 6 continents. He is also a Managing Director of Expansive Ventures (**http://expansive.vc**), an early-stage venture firm, and the Founding Member of **TheFunded.com**, an online community of over 20,000 CEOs to research, rate, and review funding sources worldwide. In addition, Adeo serves on the Board of the X PRIZE foundation, a non-profit chartered to inspire human achievements through competition. Expansive Ventures is the ninth company that Adeo has founded or built, four of which were acquired and four of which are still operating.

Adeo is widely regarded as an expert on startups and venture capital, and a global advocate for founder rights, with numerous appearances in The New York Times, The Wall Street Journal, Wired Magazine, NBC News, ABC News, BusinessWeek, Fortune, Forbes, Time Magazine, Entrepreneur, CNN, and more.

Introduction

Ideas have always fascinated me. This is perhaps not surprising, given that my name Naveen in Sanskrit means *new*. However, this fascination has also prompted me to help hundreds of budding entrepreneurs, in the past ten years alone, to understand how to transform their innovations into viable businesses. This occurred through my position as co-founder of Compassites, as well as my association with the Founder Institute, for whom I direct mentoring and other programs in Bangalore, India.

Throughout this time I've been grappling with the question that lies at the heart of this book: How do I find that one winning business idea? To help illustrate how I arrived at the answer, let me share a real-life experience with you.

One of the places in the world I travel to frequently is the Bay Area of California. That's not surprising, given how much the ecosystem we commonly refer to as *Silicon Valley* has in common with my home base of Bangalore. On one such visit I was due to meet an aspiring entrepreneur who had been introduced to me virtually by a mutual friend living in Sunnyvale. Thanks to the wonders of modern technology, not least the ability to Google each other, this man—let's call him Sunil—had got to know quite a bit about me before we met. With a high degree of trust and respect already established, Sunil was ready to present to me his "winning" idea.

Here's what he told me: "When we get together during dinner time, we all watch television. When the commercials come on, that's when everyone strikes up a conversation. My idea is to make the television automatically mute itself as soon as the commercials come on and resume the volume when the commercials end. That way viewers don't even have to bother pressing a button and they can utilize time to chat without any background noise or disturbance."

Now, what would you have told Sunil about the likelihood that he could build a successful, sustainable business from this idea?

One thing that might have occurred to you is that television networks earn considerable revenues from TV commercials. Therefore advertisers would not be happy with an idea that enabled people who were buying new televisions, or even purchasing a separate gadget, to be able to automatically mute the TV's sound the moment the commercials came on. You would be right in thinking that this is one of the reasons why this kind of idea has not yet been adopted. Not least because of the considerable resistance there would be from thousands of organizations that advertise on television every year, not to mention the PR and advertising companies that support them.

Another thought you might have had is why anyone would bother automating this process when you already have a remote that comes with your television, allowing you to mute anything you don't wish to hear. Again, that's a valid objection to Sunil's concept. Except, of course, many people will always pay for the convenience of innovations that save them even seconds of time. For example, as drivers we've been used to using physical maps to help us get from A to B. Then came GPS and other "on board" systems that simplified this process even more. The Google Car, which allows you to feed in data about your destination and perhaps also your preferred route, is simply taking this to the next level. So, there is no doubt in my mind that consumers will always pay for extra convenience.

Evaluating Ideas

Within minutes of listening to Sunil talk about his plan to transform his idea into a viable commercial reality, I was able to come to a conclusion about the likelihood of his success. I told him that while I thought his idea could be very useful, it was not feasible as the basis for building a business.

Sunil was astonished, not just by my reaction but also the speed at which I was able to evaluate his idea. In just a few minutes I was able to determine that he would not be able to sustain a business on the back of it. I did so by using a model that I am going to share with you in this book, which was developed thanks to my ongoing partnership with ideators in India and Silicon Valley, as part of my responsibilities as co-founder of Compassites.

What I discovered during my discussions about ideation, incubation, and the navigation of new business with prospective investors and partners in California in particular, was the considerable challenge of how best to describe Compassites' core competence. What I needed was an easy, understandable way to articulate how our company could quickly and accurately validate the hundreds of ideas we were being presented with every year.

Just to give you a sense of this, let's say that during any single year our company is offered or has to review 100 ideas. (In actual fact, we receive many more than that.) Imagine the time it takes to evaluate each of these ideas individually, from whether the person pitching the idea has the ability or passion necessary to execute it successfully, or can even be part of that execution, to whether the timing for such an idea is optimal. But most important to *our* business was the fact that there was going to be no point investing so much intellectual capital, time and money in ventures that had no chance of becoming viable, sustainable companies.

I soon realized, as I spoke with the people we wanted to give *us* money and to invest in *our* success, that if we didn't have a reliable model with which to evaluate the countless opportunities we were being presented with day in, day out, then we'd all be old and gray before we could bring any of these business ideas to market.

In order to explain to our U.S. funders and potential customers how Compassites could foster entrepreneurship from ideas that had the best chance of becoming viable, sustainable companies, I needed a compelling

metaphor. This is how I came up with what I call the Rose Model, since a rose is a wonderful way to describe all the basic elements of entrepreneurship.

Roses are related traditionally with love and passion, but they also have painful thorns. One of the painful things that aspiring entrepreneurs have to deal with, I have found, is the extent to which they can translate their expectations about entrepreneurship, and what it takes to build a sustainable business, into a *reality*. Few of the entrepreneurs I've come across have said they wanted to be an entrepreneur purely to make money. This is a good thing because, to my mind, this should not be the only driving force for embarking on an entrepreneurial venture. But in many cases the aspiring founders I've been asked to coach and advise have not given sufficient thought to their true purpose, or the practicalities they will face before embarking on this path.

Why Entrepreneurs Fail

The entrepreneurial journey brings with it a considerable change in lifestyle. When you work for an established organization you are used to certain things. You know how much money you will bring home each month; how many hours you are expected to work. You are entitled to a certain number of paid holidays and your employer may make contributions toward healthcare costs and pension plans. Entrepreneurs, on the other hand, work around the clock and at least in the early years cannot expect the same kind of security. These are just some of the challenges I have found that many aspiring entrepreneurs are *not* tuned into. Since everything is down to you (and your co-founders if this is applicable), you have to take charge and use tact to solve these challenges. This journey doesn't move forward unless there is planning and a methodological approach.

One of the statistics I see frequently is that the success rate is high for those who have started their entrepreneurial journey again, *after failing in their first venture*. It appears that failure has helped to iron out the false expectations and myths about entrepreneurship that the person perhaps held when they first embarked on this journey. It is these false expectations and myths that serve to contribute to the depressing statistics such as the one reported by Harvard Business School, that the likelihood of entrepreneurs succeeding with their first venture is something like 18 per cent.[2] Even that is an optimistic figure, since in my direct experience the outcome is even more disheartening. Only one per cent of entrepreneurial ideas reach the level of a successful, sustainable enterprise. And, as Adeo Ressi points out in the Foreword to this book, only .4 per cent or four in 1,000 create businesses with global impact.

Why are we faced with these depressing statistics? I'll say it again:

> Because most aspiring entrepreneurs fail to realize
> that every good idea doesn't necessarily have the
> potential to become a viable business.

Nevertheless, by using the Rose Model I developed we could quickly and easily validate ideas. This showed our investors and prospective partners that Compassites had a methodology for qualifying whether or not ideas shared by aspiring entrepreneurs were capable of sustaining successful entrepreneurial ventures.

I will go through Sunil's idea in more detail in Chapter One, showing how the Rose Model helped me to quickly assess this idea as unsuitable for building a business. For now, let me conclude the rest of the story by outlining how I left things with him.

As I told Sunil, while I thought his idea lacked what was needed to become a sustainable business, it was a useful feature that was certainly patentable. It might even be something that he could choose to explore as a hobby. Then again, perhaps he could find another use for this idea that might benefit existing start-up founders who were working on a business model that needed this kind of functionality? When we parted ways,

---

2 Business Insider, Why Some Startups Succeed and Others Fail: 10 Fascinating Harvard Findings, http://read.bi/1OO76jN (accessed December 6, 2015)

Sunil said he was happy that he hadn't gone ahead and started a business before speaking with me. He was convinced by my brief explanation of the Rose Model and our discussion that I had not only saved him time, effort and money but he was excited that he still had an avenue or two to explore, with respect to patenting or applying his idea to other contexts.

Who This Book Benefits (or May Not)

In my opinion, no idea is a bad idea. The objective of this book is both to increase the success rate of start-ups by overturning the current high failure rate of entrepreneurial ventures, AND to help demolish the risk barriers that hold back many people from contributing to these economically important and personally fulfilling activities.

What this book is NOT about is how to come up with ideas in the first place. It is not a book about creativity *per se,* or how to become more creative or innovative. If, like one group of MBA students I spoke to, you would be inclined to raise your hand to the question: "How many of you think you CANNOT come up with good ideas?" then this book might be a poor investment for you at this point. This is because FOUND is focused on evaluating, from any number of so-called "winning ideas" that you already have, the ONE idea that could become a reality in terms of supporting a viable business.

Having said that, you may still find this book is of value to you in understanding that not every idea can or should become a commercial reality. (Remember, it could be patented or become the basis of an absorbing side venture or hobby.) Knowing this, you could find your mind becomes freer after reading this book, which would then allow you to come up with lot more new ideas.

Measurable Results

Having ideas is not really the major challenge here. After all, how many times have you felt aroused by passion, curiosity, or even anger, and found that these emotions provoked in you a desire to try and provide a solution to a known problem? It is these kinds of feeling that best fuel the ingenuity of individuals. But, again, that doesn't necessarily mean everyone should try and build businesses from such efforts. As a personal passion it doesn't matter if your idea doesn't catch on, although it's a bonus if it does. However, the core issue that this book addresses is how to recognize the one idea, out of many ideas you may have, that is most likely to become a *serious business*.

In many cases, I have found that people feel disappointed or that they have failed in some way when their business doesn't yield the expected results. Whereas if they had only recognized it was never going to be more than a pastime in the first place and had no other expectations than that, perhaps it would have made them happier with their efforts.

The good news for you is two-fold: In reading this book, you are obviously someone who recognizes you need a disciplined approach toward validating an idea before launching it as a business, and you can be confident that the process I am about to share with you will help you achieve *measurable* results.

Through my work as the director of the Founder Institute in Bangalore, India, I have facilitated ideation boot camps and other programs where people have learned the FOUND framework and applied the same knowledge to their businesses that you will find within these pages. While it is one thing to be able to evaluate an idea, you also need a step-by-step process that can help you increase your chances of identifying what a "winning" idea (in the sense of sustaining a business), looks like to begin with. The FOUND process you are about to learn is not theory-based, but draws from the experience and understanding of many already-established entrepreneurs who have built *real* companies that have stood the test of time.

As a point of comparison, in the last five years the Founder Institute has helped something like 90 percent of the ideas brought to them by entrepreneurs to become commercial realities. Almost 72 percent of those businesses are thriving, and over 42 percent of them have received external funding. This is a complete turnaround of the pyramid I mentioned earlier, whereby typically just one percent of ideas succeed as entrepreneurial ventures while the other 99 per cent don't.

Intrapreneurship and Entrepreneurship

What I am often asked is whether the process outlined in this book applies only to entrepreneurs, or whether it can be adopted successfully by employees to increase their *intrapreneurship*. By *intrapreneurs* I mean people who are working within an enterprise to develop further ideas for that organization. My answer to this question is a resounding *Yes!* The application of the process is the same, it is always about validating ideas and conducting the necessary market research, irrespective of whether you are an entrepreneur or an intrapreneur. The only key difference concerns the sponsors. In an entrepreneurial initiative the founder is the core sponsor for transforming their idea into a commercial reality, as well as the person responsible to their outside investors, if they have them. On the other hand, with an intrapreneurial initiative, the company in which the individual works is the sponsor. This is where adopting the approach contained within the pages of this book will not only be invaluable to the company, but also to the ideator's own career.

I am sure you are familiar with the vicious circle where, oftentimes, people stop taking ideas to management because they get very little or no encouragement to bring them to fruition. On the other hand, every organization is hungry for those people who not only come up with good ideas and are willing to take ownership to execute them, but demonstrate that they have done their due diligence and are presenting the company *only* ideas that have been validated first. With both the Rose Model and the FOUND process at your fingertips you can be one of those all-too-rare individuals.

How To Use This Book

My intention with this book is to present you with all the information you need to execute the FOUND approach for yourself, as well as to have the Rose Model at your fingertips for those occasions when you need to make a rapid assessment of an idea. Throughout each chapter you will find prompts that ask you to stop and think about your own ideas and aspirations, as well as real-life stories that will hopefully inspire you to create your own long-term entrepreneurial success.

* ***Chapter One,*** *The Rose Model* revisits Sunil's TV muting idea to outline the Rose model I mentioned briefly earlier. This can be used to help you further validate each of the five steps in the overall process, called FOUND.

* ***Chapters Two through Six.*** Each of these five chapters follows the same format: I introduce and fully explain *one* of the iterative steps that you need to take in order to arrive at a single executable idea that could support a business. It is here that you will find evidence for why each step will be invaluable to you, together with concrete examples provided by some of the mentors with whom I am associated through the Founder Institute, both in India and other countries:

Chapter Two:	**F**ree-Flow
Chapter Three:	**O**rientate
Chapter Four:	**U**nearth
Chapter Five:	**N**egotiate
Chapter Six:	**D**etermine/Decide.

* ***Chapter Seven*** is entitled *Navigating The Matrix*. This introduces a further refinement of the FOUND process, with a grid that can help you identify the market for your product or service, and how ready that market is likely to be to receive your idea.

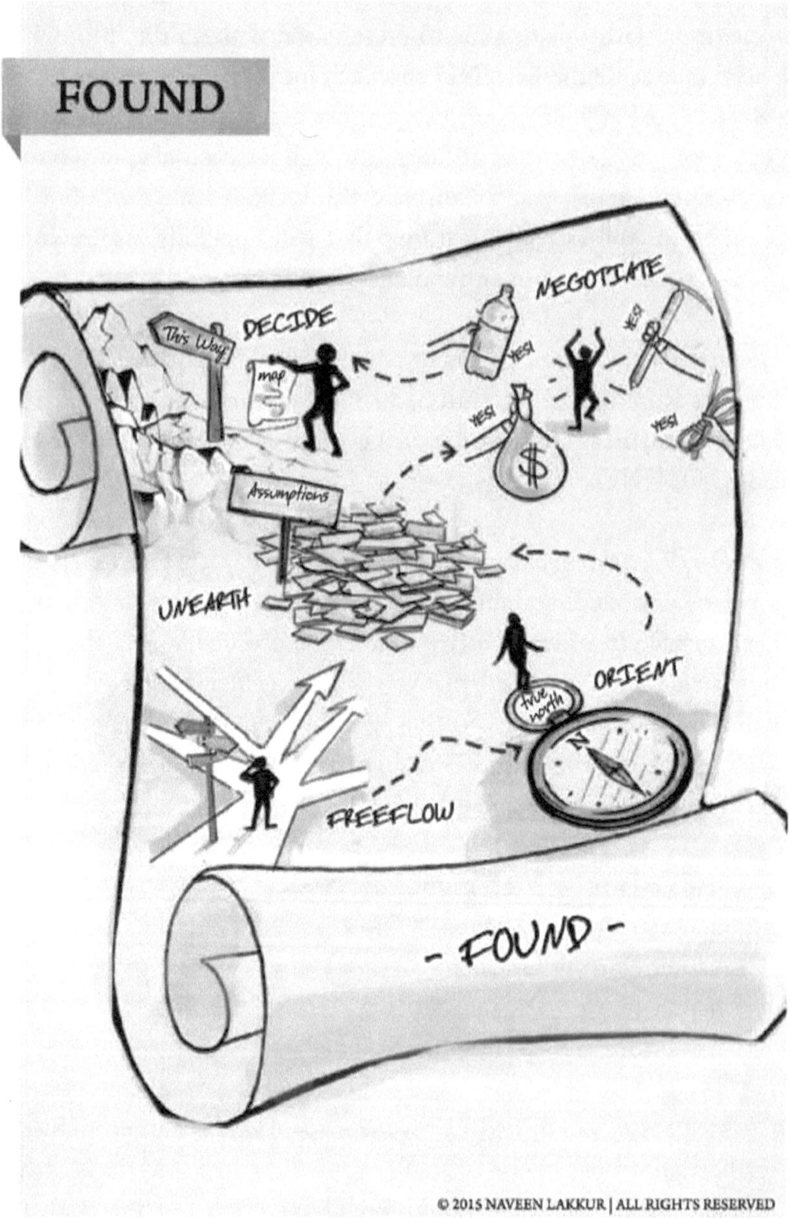

FOUND

DECIDE
NEGOTIATE
This Way
map
YES!
YES!
YES!
YES!
$
Assumptions
UNEARTH
true north
ORIENT
N
FREEFLOW
- FOUND -

- ***Chapter Eight**, Ideas Unlimited, Opportunities Countless* is the section in which Dr. Liz asked me a number of questions to which I could offer next-steps advice. Reading each of these will help you move forward and make your concept a *reality* rather than just let it remain another good idea that never sees the light of day.

- ***Chapter Nine**, Been There, Done That!* contains six stories shared by already-successful entrepreneurs, that illustrate the steps they have taken to establish their own successful enterprises.

Before We Begin…

When you choose to answer the question, "How do I find that one winning business idea?" you are doing more, much more, than fulfilling a deep personal need to create something for yourself. There is a quote I am fond of which states: "Great minds share ideas, average minds share experiences, and low minds complain." The world needs more great minds, don't you agree?

What I have concluded from being involved for so many years in the ideation process is that we must make "great minds" part of the broader culture. We desperately need more people who will help to build our economies by coming up with innovative ways to solve our challenges. After all, there are countless problems in the world that need solutions and I think you will agree that there is no dearth of ideas. It is what we *do*, however, with these ideas that is so fundamentally important.

None of this is simply a profession for me. The work I do is my passion. What I have found to be particularly gratifying is how, by directing our conscious efforts toward focusing on ideas that can truly sustain a business, all that positive energy benefits more than the individual entrepreneur: It serves the world.

Do we continue to do what so many failed entrepreneurs have done in the past, and continue to do, by becoming so excited by our ideas that we try to launch businesses on the back of them without validating the

concept, thereby ending up wasting all that time, money and effort? Or do we adopt the disciplined, proven approach that is outlined in this book and develop commercial realities that can build sustainable economies for years to come?

If you are willing to embrace the second approach, I now invite you to please join me on this fascinating, life-changing journey.

Chapter One

The Rose Model

What is the first thing you think of when you read the word "rose"? For many people it's the petals, from which the rose gets its fragrance, texture and color. What we tend not to immediately focus on are the thorns and the core or "bud." This is similar to what happens when I, and most of the venture capitalists I speak with, ask entrepreneurs to describe their winning idea. And it is the key reason why those entrepreneurs don't get funded. Because their innovation is not something that can sustain an ongoing business.

In this chapter, I'm going to outline the whole of the Rose Model, mentioned earlier in the Introduction. While this model is not a part of the FOUND process that you will learn throughout the rest of the book, what it represents and offers is a quick and easy way for you (as it does for me), to evaluate a single idea. Explaining the Rose Model will also help to shift your mindset to that of the individual or group that you want to persuade to invest in your business. Or, if you are not looking for outside funding, to protect you from wasting your own time, money and effort on an idea that does not have what's necessary to sustain your business over the long-term.

You may remember that Sunil's idea centered around a device that would ensure a TV set went mute the moment the commercials came on, and would resume volume when they were over. That, in Sunil's mind, would

17

help facilitate the conversations that frequently take place when these breaks in TV programs and movies occur. Let's consider the three parts of the rose—the thorns, the core or "bud," and the petals—with respect to this suggested innovation, leaving aside any of the other objections I raised in the Introduction.

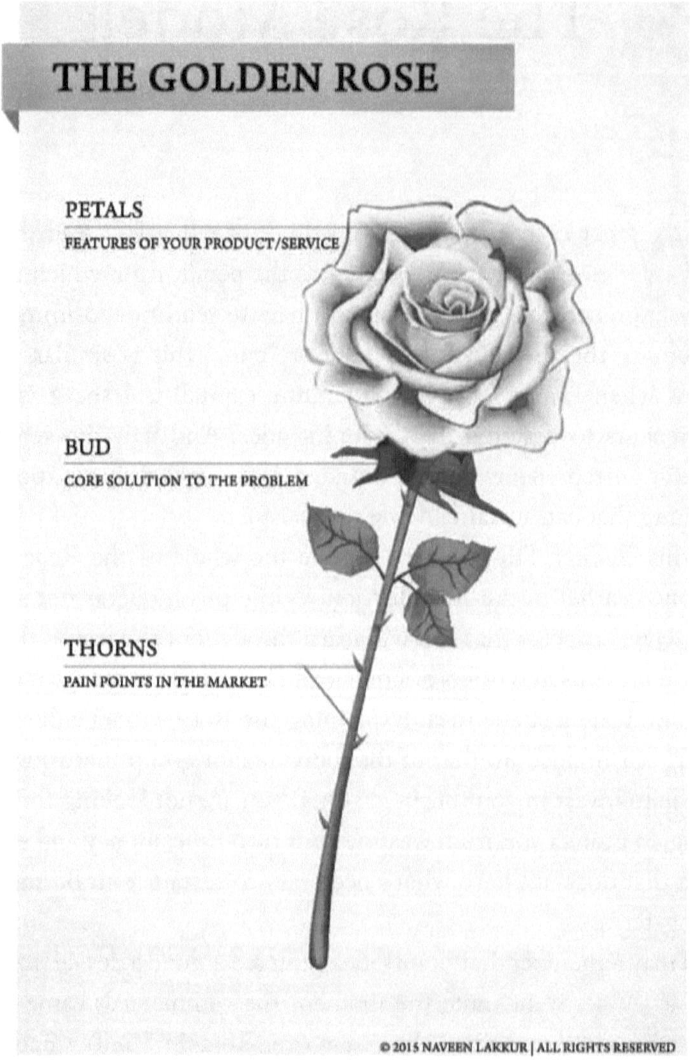

Thorny Pain Points

Whether or not you grow them yourself you are probably aware that as beautiful as roses are, most of the varieties you buy have thorns along their stems. I think of these thorns as analogous to the pain points that your customer or client have with respect to the solution you are trying to offer them. The higher the degree of "pain" that is felt by your market, the greater their willingness to buy into your solution. In addition to that, the more different kinds of pain points that are being experienced already by your clients or customers, the better this is for you, because there are going to be any number of reasons why they would be attracted to your idea.

So, the first thing that Sunil needed to do was to realistically assess and confirm, beyond the shadow of a doubt, that the imagined pain points he believed were being experienced by potential clients for his TV muting device were strong and deep enough to bring him sufficient business. (This is where the research you will learn more about in Chapter Four is vital to the future success of your potential business.) For now, let's imagine that these pain points are real and move on to the next feature of the rose.

Core/Bud and Petals

Having determined the nature and extent of those pain points that will draw potential clients and prospects to your idea, let's now look more closely at the solution to the problem, because this is where Sunil's idea really broke down. What he was suggesting to me is what I would describe as a "petal": a feature or functionality with which many aspiring entrepreneurs become seduced into thinking they have something that can be transformed into a business. Here's the problem with trying to build a business on the bells and whistles or "petals" of an otherwise solid idea: anyone can come along and copy it.

Think about it. Imagine that Sunil had based his business on this TV muting device. By the time he had successfully patented it, someone else could have come along having either developed the exact same thing or

added even greater functionality. There is no security for an entrepreneurial venture when its future depends only on features and functionality.

That is why so many entrepreneurs get turned down for external funding, when Venture Capitalists (VCs) only hear them talk about the features and functionality of their idea. VCs know that these are not enough to support a fully-fledged business.

> There is no security for an entrepreneurial venture when its future depends only on features and functionality.

For any business to have a strong foundation and to grow, as is the case with our imagined rose, it is essential that it has a bud or core. Without that, there is nothing to hold the petals (or features) together. Indeed, without the bud there is no rose at all. And that is what this book has been written to help you do—to provide an innovative solution to a market problem that has a strong enough foundation with which to sustain a business over as many years as you choose to work at it.

That is what I communicated to Sunil and the reason why he left our short meeting grateful not to be spending the time, money and effort on an idea that would not bring about the required return on those considerable personal investments. When it comes to evaluating any idea, first I look for the thorns. Where are the pain points in the market, whether it be an individual customers in the case of a potential B2C (business to consumer) business, or corporate clients in case of B2B (business to business)? If there are no pain points, then it's unlikely that your idea is going to become a successful business.

As long as we can establish a need, and it is one that people will pay money for, as nothing currently like it is available or is likely to come about through someone *copying* the idea, then we know that our rose contains a viable core or "bud." Only then do I consider the specific features or functionalities ("petals") of the product or service that is being pitched to me.

No "Bad" Ideas

Let me reiterate a point I made earlier: I don't think in terms of "bad ideas," only ideas that have not been *categorized* properly. Indeed, I've been frequently fascinated by the ideas and innovations of many of the aspiring entrepreneurs I've met over the past 20 years. Some of them have had no intention of creating a business out of their ideas, for which I would say there is no impact. But let me help you understand this concept of *categorization* with an illustration.

I imagine you've likely visited a Starbucks or similar coffee house and have had the benefit of using those cardboard sleeves that are inserted onto each cup of hot coffee or tea to act as an insulator to prevent your fingers getting burned. This is a classic case of someone who's had a good idea that was then patented and commercialized by someone else. Imagine if the original innovator had decided to go into business manufacturing these cardboard sleeves, without having given consideration as to how they might be used or who would buy them. You can see how, in that case, it would be difficult for such a business to survive. By categorizing themselves as the patentee of the idea and allowing it to be commercialized by different vendors with direct links to the people who could most benefit (i.e., purchasers of hot tea and coffee), then at least the original innovator could receive royalties for each sleeve that is being sold. In this particular example, the patented idea served its purpose by earning revenues from the various vendors who commercialized it. In many respects this was the only way in which I could see Sunil making money from his TV muting device idea.

Thorns = Pain Points
Core/Bud = Your competitive solution
(with a readily identifiable, paying market)
Petals = Features and Functionality

What's Next?

This, then, is the Rose Model[3], one that entrepreneurs and VCs I have worked with find quick and easy to understand and have used themselves to help evaluate ideas. It is a model you should employ when you need to decide whether or not you have a concept that you could build into a sustainable business.

But, as most highly creative people know, finding an idea is the least of your problems. There are ideas aplenty, the challenge is in whittling them down—evaluating one against the other—in order to arrive at that single, winning idea. That is what is covered in the rest of this book.

In the chapters that follow, I am going to encourage you to begin with so many ideas that their numbers are in double digits. How do you choose which among them to evaluate, so that you are not scattering your energies over too wide a field of activity? After all, you don't want to be spending all your time just trying to work out which is the *best* idea to lead with. You want to focus most of your efforts on building a business.

And once you have evaluated a number of those ideas, how do you determine which ones warrant further research? How might you go about doing that?

Having done your due diligence, researched your market and convinced yourself of the likelihood that there is sufficient value in your idea to build and sustain a business, what comes next? What is the penultimate activity that all entrepreneurs should undertake—but few do—before reaching the point at which you know, *beyond a shadow of a doubt*, that you have an idea to pursue that will be the foundation of a successful, long-term business? This is what you will learn and know how to do by the time you reach the end of this book.

---

3   Inspired by the "Sunflower Model" of world renowned entrepreneur, Rob Ryan, the founder of Entrepreneur America Mentors' bootcamps: https://en.wikipedia.org/wiki/Rob_Ryan_(entrepreneur)

In Chapter Six (Determine/Decide) you will read how Rajeev Pathak, the founder of eDream Edusoft based in Bangalore, India applied the FOUND process to help him determine and develop his disruptive technology start-up for the education industry.

But first, let's work our way systematically through the FOUND acronym. Starting with F for Free-Flow.

Free-Flow

The sayings of prolific U.S. inventor, businessman, and co-founder of the General Electric Company (GE), Thomas Alva Edison, are well known and especially pertinent to fellow entrepreneurs. You are probably already well aware of this quote, attributed to Edison during the time he was trying to find a suitable material to act as the filament for an electric light bulb:

> "I have not failed. I've just found
> 10,000 ways that won't work."

But, have you ever stopped to wonder how Edison was able to take such a balanced view of "failure," such that every attempt of his which did not succeed was seen as one step closer to success? Edison's mindset is extremely instructive to entrepreneurs for the simple fact that it is contrary to the way most people think. Let me explain what I mean by that.

In my experience, most aspiring entrepreneurs get too caught up in their "big idea," hence they fail to identify the larger problem that it is meant to solve. If you have read anything at all about Edison's life you will realize that, despite being largely "uneducated" by modern standards, he had an insatiable fascination for the workings of the universe. Edison didn't set out to create a light bulb. What motivated him was solving a problem that no one had yet accomplished: the elimination of darkness by choice. That is, through developing the incandescent light bulb, Edison gave everyone the power to do whatever they chose to do, irrespective of whether it was dark or not, and at the flip of a switch rather than the more tedious, and dangerous, process of lighting a gas lamp.

> *Most aspiring entrepreneurs get too caught up in their "big idea," hence they fail to identify the larger problem that it is meant to solve.*

Consider how, by focusing on the *problem* rather than the *idea* for solving this problem, Edison was able to remain motivated, even though it took him 10,000 or more attempts using various different ways, before he was able to come up with an effective carbon-based filament for his light bulb. Had Edison been obsessed only with his idea, each failure would have undoubtedly sapped his motivation. As it was, Edison's passion had limitless possibilities and he was able to try out lots of different ideas in the search for a viable solution. These limitless possibilities came about because of the powerful context he had set originally, to empower people to eliminate darkness by choice.

Things To Think About

We are now in the first phase of the ideation journey. Here are a few important things to think about and adopt as you move forward.

> *Being obsessed with an idea only makes it more difficult to remain motivated when things don't work out as we imagine. Being obsessed with the problem you wish to solve ensures that you remain flexible about where new ideas might come from.*

- Go crazy in generating as many new ideas as you can at this stage. Allow your thoughts to "free-flow." Think: the more the merrier.
- Maintain an open mind. There should be no resistance for new ideas to emerge. No idea is taboo. Reject nothing, as wild as it might first appear.
- Don't start to analyze your ideas in terms of their practicality or viability—that comes later.
- Remember, it's not necessary that you should generate all the ideas by yourself. Crowd source them. Know that everyone is born creative and has the ability to produce fresh ideas.
- Listen to the problems or needs of your prospective market. Some of the best ideas have manifested themselves because of keen listening.
- As an aspiring entrepreneur, try and generate at least 25 ideas during this initial phase, *even if you already have one that interests you* and you think it could be the "winner." (Which brings us back to the second bullet point: Keep an open mind!)

Being obsessed with an idea only makes it more difficult to remain motivated when things don't work out as we imagine. Being obsessed with the problem you wish to solve ensures that you remain flexible about where new ideas might come from.

As you will have gathered when reading words like "obsessed" and "passionate" in the section above, there must be emotion associated with whatever problem you wish to solve. In Edison's case it was his intense curiosity that propelled him from success to success, resulting in his record of over 1,000 successful U.S. patents, not counting the hundreds more that he applied for that were not successful.

If you are still at the stage where you don't have a specific idea to pursue, here's a clue as to how you might find one. Think about what problems or challenges you or the people you know have come across that have elicited a strong emotion. To show you how this works, here are three brief case studies, each of them similar as they focus on the theme of transportation, but whose solutions came about because of a different underlying emotion.

In keeping with what you have just read about Edison, the first case study concerns curiosity, the second shows how passion can be the impetus for innovative ideas, and the third tells the story of how anger led to a venture that, eight years after being founded, was sold for USD $100 million.

CURIOSITY: Brompton Bike Hire (U.K.)

Although Brompton had become a growing concern in the mid-1980s, some thirty years later this maker of premium, hand-made folding bicycles based in West London, England faced growing competition from bigger businesses and was at risk of being out-priced and out-produced.

Brompton's leaders knew they needed to be bold in finding an idea that could help them grow their brand by introducing new customers to their uniquely hinged bicycle models. After all, the Brompton team had been "green" long before it became fashionable. Their bicycles provided the means of getting from A to B without causing any harm to the environment, unlike the emissions of cars and motorcycles, but they had the additional advantage of being highly portable. The bikes could be folded and easily lifted onto other forms of transportation, like trains and buses.

Curious about the concept of setting up docking stations at which people could hire a Brompton bike and experience their value first-hand at low cost, the company reached out to a number of potential collaborators. These included universities with large campuses, where students could reach their classes more easily without having to walk, local authorities who wanted to provide visitors with a fun, energizing way of seeing the sights without having to buy train or bus tickets, and operators like Virgin Trains where commuters could pick up a bike, take it on the train then ride it to their offices without having to worry about being stuck in traffic jams.

Today, Brompton Bike Hire has gone from that basic idea—stemming from a curiosity as to how the company might introduce a premium bicycle product to more potential customers—to a successful business strategy.

As Harry Scrope, who heads up the initiative says: "Brompton Bike Hire provides a flexible solution and environmentally friendly commuting tool for fitness-focused people who might not otherwise be aware of our brand. Through hiring these fantastic products they can discover, at very little cost, how the Brompton folding bike fits into their lives and hopefully soon discover that they cannot live without it."

In Brompton's case, this curiosity was fueled by a passion for their products and the lifestyle they offer. Indeed, it's often hard to separate curiosity from passion.

So let's look now at another case study, this time focused on how two Indian software engineers turned their passion for transportation into a socially-focused solution for Indian commuters and the drivers who serve them.

PASSION: Autowale (Pune, India)

The co-founders of Autowale (pronounced auto-wah-ley) don't just share a passion for technology, they also feel very emotional about traffic generally.

In Janardan Prasad's case, being slightly asthmatic, he hates the pollution caused by traffic and whenever possible avoids driving in congested areas. His business partner, Mukesh Jha on the other hand, loves to be on the road whether by car or motorcycle.

Recognizing that traffic is a big problem in Indian cities, including Pune where they both live and founded Autowale, these two entrepreneurs—alums of the Indian Institute of Techology Kanpur (IITK)—set about channeling their passion to find a solution to the everyday Indian commute. Recognizing this issue was huge to begin with, they selected a specific portion of the commute in India, one involving almost 20 per cent of trips: the auto rickshaw service. There are nearly five million auto rickshaws on roads in India, but most of the time you'll find these drivers sitting playing cards, or driving around streets, not knowing when or where their next customer might come from.

From the customer's perspective, the current system also presented a problem. What if you have a train or plane to catch and want to avail yourself of this cheaper alternative of going to the station or airport by hailing one of these three-wheeled, open sided taxis, rather than calling a cab? You might stand on the street corner for a while without any auto rickshaws driving past. Or a driver might stop but decide the route you want him to take is out of his way and he refuses to take you. Both scenarios amount to undesirable, costly delays.

Janardan and Mukesh were passionate about solving this impasse between drivers who were using up empty miles with no passengers, and customers who couldn't access an auto rickshaw on demand.

What they ended up doing (and you'll read more of the Autowale story later, in Chapter Four), was to develop their own proprietary predictive software so that customers can now book an auto rickshaw via an app, the Web or by phoning the Autowale call center. These customers then have the advantage of a convenient, inexpensive ride at a time that suits them and know that because of the training Autowale gives, their drivers will be courteous and honest. Drivers, too, have benefited hugely from being part of the Autowale service, with many of them seeing an increase in income of 100 per cent or more.

As Janardan Prasad says: "We love to play with technology, but we don't want to use technology in a way that only produces a cool, sci-fi product kind of thing. We want to do something with it that will impact real lives."

That's passion!

Passion can take on other forms, of course, and one of them is disappointment, leading to anger. And it was this so-called "negative" emotion that helped drive the founders of redBus to become India's largest bus ticketing company.

DISAPPOINTMENT: redBus (India)

In 2005, 25-year old Phanindra Sama was working as a software engineer in Bangalore, Karnataka, and wanted to return to his home town in Andra Pradesh—an overnight travel by bus—in order to celebrate the festival of Diwali with his family. The trouble was, he couldn't find an available bus ticket. Despite visiting one travel agent after another in the city, no one was able to help him and he found the search for available seats to be time-consuming and tedious. Aside from wasting all that time and energy on what should have been a simple exercise, Phanindra was angered by the fact that while Expedia had been making flights available to consumers since 1996, there was no system in place for making the availability of bus tickets readily accessible to travelers in India.

It was this emotion—anger—that prompted Phanindra to round up his fellow engineers and alums of the Birla Institute of Technology and Science in Pillani (BITS) to create an online solution. This worked out extremely well, since all of these friends were new to Bangalore and other than the time they spent working for multi-national corporations like IBM and Texas Instruments, there wasn't much else to occupy them at the weekends.

As redBus co-founder Charan Padmaraju is quoted as saying in Shereen Bhan's book *Young Turks: Inspiring Stories of Tech Entrepreneurs* (Random

House India, 2014): "It was all about building something that would be useful to someone. It looked exciting and different—we made trips to bus operators to find out what their pain points were and built the software to solve those."

For more on the redBus story, I recommend you read *Young Turks* as the journey from the inception of the idea to the launch of the company is highly instructive for any entrepreneur, not least when it comes to focusing on whose pain points or "thorns" (those of customers as well as bus operators), to address first. But you have to ask yourself whether such an idea might have come to fruition had it not been for the frustration and anger that Phanindra Sama experienced while trying to get home for Diwali.

* * *

To sum up the F of the FOUND process:

Being obsessed with the problem you want to solve, rather than remaining fixated on a single solution, is the major difference between success and failure in the entrepreneurial world. The more you explore stories such as the three shared with you in this chapter, the more you will discover that often there is an underlying *emotion* to an entrepreneur's desire to solve something. Either it's a problem they have experienced directly (preferably), or have heard of others experiencing, and feel passionate about solving it.

If you are still at the stage of trying to find a viable business idea, trying looking at this challenge from a different angle. At what point have you felt curiosity, passion, anger, or any other emotion when experiencing a problem? How might that propel you into generating new ideas for finding a solution?

Now it's time to look more closely at how many of these free-flowing ideas are a good fit for *you*.

Orientate

One of the biggest issues I see among the entrepreneurs I have mentored over the years, that causes them to fail in their desire to translate their ideas into sustainable businesses, is considering their idea as separate from themselves. For successful entrepreneurs, however, their relationship with their business is like that of a marriage.

Now that you have an emotionally fueled idea that you want to progress, it's time to do a personality fit. This new, potentially "winning" idea might sound interesting to you and it might be focused on a big problem. But here's the key question: How will you feel about it 5, 10, 15 years from now? For successful entrepreneurs, their businesses are part and parcel of their lives—extensions of themselves, if you like. This is an inseparable dynamic that you will become increasingly aware of as you read this book, as it is a theme running through all the case studies including that of Rajeev Pathak, whose story you will come across in Chapter Six (Determine/Decide).

In the meantime, let me illustrate this with a brief story of my own that shows the links between many different aspects of my life.

CASE STUDY: Naveen and Online Marketplace

The latest entrepreneurial trend is the online marketplace, especially aggregating local service providers. I frequently get invited to be a mentor for these ventures or to become a co-founder. There are online marketplaces for lifestyle services, providing one-click convenience for anyone with everyday lifestyle needs. These range from finding a health advisor, a real estate consultant, an investment expert, a tutor or after-school workshop for children, an evening class where you can learn a new hobby or skill, or someone who can create a dream vacation package for you.

Here's why this is a concept that I'm so passionate about.

For the first 20 years of my life, I was not only studying at school and college but I was also supporting my father in running our family business, a grocery store in a physical marketplace where people would come to buy their daily needs.

After I graduated with my engineering degree, I spent the next 20 years working in the technology field, helping to build companies that could leverage that technology to provide global solutions.

When I was originally introduced to the idea behind some of these online marketplaces with which I've been associated, it wasn't hard to see the fit. Because when it comes down to it, the online marketplace is simply a combination of these two earlier experiences and passions of mine. What we have done is simply to take the idea of a physical marketplace and put it online, using technology to bring together service providers and consumers in an innovative way.

I see this orientation completing my life. Everything I have experienced, the areas in which I am most skilled and the passion I have for simplifying people's lives through the use of technology, are melded together in this exciting new entrepreneurial opportunity. In short, nothing I have ever done has gone to waste; it is all being leveraged.

> Your big idea and who you are as a unique individual are two separate entities that must come together as if they represented one life.

The Idea(l) Life

Whether or not you have undertaken it yourself, you are presumably familiar with the concept of marriage. Which is a good thing, since marriage is analogous to the relationship you should intend to have with your business. Successful marriages, to my mind, are less about two ideal people coming together but about two people with different mindsets wishing to lead an *ideal life* together. In the same sense, your big idea and who you are as a unique individual are two separate entities that must come together as if they represented one life.

To further emphasize this point, it is very difficult for a passionate person to separate their personal and professional lives. That is why the concept known as "work-life balance" is nonsensical to entrepreneurs. We don't need to "balance" anything, because we see everything that we do as part of the whole of who we are.

But don't just take my word for it. Here's the perspective of one Vistage Chairman, Ivan Goldberg, who represents the worldwide organization that since 1957 has provided senior executive coaching, leadership development and business mentoring through their private peer advisory model.

Ivan Goldberg of Vistage International

Ivan Goldberg is based in the U.K., where he has been a Group Chairman for Vistage International for 24 years. During that time he has worked with many bright, intelligent and driven people whose sole aim is to achieve success in their chosen field of business. When asked about this concept of orientation and how important it is in entrepreneurial ventures, he had this to say:

"There is no question in my mind that entrepreneurs who create and sustain the most successful businesses combine great ideas with their own blend of passion, commitment, personal values and strengths. In fact, I would go so far as to say that the individuals I have seen or mentored in the past 24 years are enormously attached to their businesses, almost as if they were surrogate children, because they so strongly identify with them and have this huge emotional attachment. If there isn't that alignment— or, as Naveen refers to it, "orientation"—I can't see how it would work.

"For example, I once knew a young man who had worked in his parents' business for a number of years. A customer came into their store one day asking for a product that was a considerable improvement to what was currently available on the market. Now, this young man could have just said, "No one makes something like that," and then tried to persuade his customer to buy only what *was* available. But what he did was to *create* that improved product, based on the customer's specific need and found that—through word-of-mouth—he was able to build a business around it. Within a few years he was running an operation that turned over millions of pounds annually.

"Now, how did that happen? It came about through a combination of his innate curiosity, a strong belief in his abilities and an understanding of the market because he had worked for his parents in their business. Or, as I said earlier, that magical blend of personal characteristics and a marketable idea.

"Not surprisingly, then, I always look for this kind of orientation when I'm mentoring someone. It can never just be about making money. I always want to sense that the entrepreneur is doing what they feel is right, that it's fun to them, that they're going to enjoy it, and as a consequence will create the energy and enthusiasm that carry other people along with them.

"In fact, I live with this orientation every day myself. Once, after I'd become detached from one job, I sat down to ponder what it was I could do next. I knew I didn't want to go back to employment and have to answer to someone else, but what did I have to offer other than my inquiring mind and considerable experience? I recognized that was enough to start my own consulting practice, because even as an employee, being a mentor and guide was something I'd been doing my whole life. The alignment was there for me and it is always there among the majority of entrepreneurs I work with. Something is always driving them and that is the combination of their desire, their belief in their product or service, their ability to execute, and giving something to the world so that they are making a difference.

"There has to be a sense of purpose and no one but you can or should determine what that is. Because when it comes to measuring success and knowing when you've been successful, it's never just about making money. It's about the personal satisfaction of having built something you feel as close to as your offspring or your partner. It's about having employed people and being able to make them happy. In short, it is the fulfillment that speaks to *who you are* as well as what you *are able to do*."

Having read Ivan's wise words, I hope you are now inspired to do some more thinking and soul searching at this point. Here is a self-exploratory exercise that I recommend you go through, before moving forward.

The following five questions will help you quickly assess whether or not you are ready to live with your current business idea, if not "till death us do part," then certainly for a considerable period. Because, like any good marriage, you should be entering into this commitment with the goal of coming together, staying together, and being together for a very long time.

Exercise: Five Question Framework

Before moving forward, please be sure to search deep inside yourself for the answers to the following five questions. If, at this point, you have a single idea you are focused on, use that as the catalyst. If, however, you are still at the stage of evaluating a number of different ideas, go through this exercise with each one of them in turn. Jot your thoughts and responses down into a journal or notebook, so you can compare and contrast them later, as this is often a useful, additional thing to do.

1. **When you think about this idea (and this means not just at the beginning but all the way through this process), are you energized and excited or find yourself feeling overwhelmed or tired, like a rundown battery?**

   I'm sure you have experienced this when you are around certain people. There are those who tire us out and drain us whenever we are in their vicinity. But the special people in our lives, the ones we always enjoy being around, help us feel buoyed up by their very presence.

   This reminds me of what a comedian once said about a really great joke: that every time you hear it, and no matter how many times you do, it should make you laugh. Similarly, if every time you think about or act on your idea and it is not energizing you, then it's time to cut it loose and move on to something else. Take my word for it, it's not worth pursuing any idea that doesn't feel fulfilling to you over time.

2. **Are you ready to do whatever it takes to bring this idea from concept to reality?**

Think back to when you first dated your partner or perhaps came across someone you really wanted to get to know. Maybe you were a meat eater and they were vegetarian and you happily made changes to your diet so that eating together was more pleasurable to you both. Or maybe they smoked and you didn't and you expressed your concerns about their health and yours in breathing second-hand smoke. Perhaps as a consequence you helped them "kick the habit," by supporting them through the challenges of quitting cigarettes.

When we embark on new relationships that are important to us there are always pains or challenges—compromises to be made—as well as many pleasures. The same holds true when it comes to your relationship with your business idea. Certainly it won't all be plain sailing, but there should be enough excitement generated and you should feel sufficiently motivated to willingly adjust your expectations to meet the needs of these new circumstances.

3. **Are you moving forward NOW with this idea, or just thinking about it?**

Again, to use the dating and marriage analogy, imagine what would have happened if you had just *thought* about the wonderful time you could have with your partner or that special person that came to mind in the previous question. Nothing would have happened, right? If you want to move forward with any worthwhile relationship you have to take action. Perhaps by first inviting them for a coffee or a meal, then gradually moving toward spending longer periods of time together. Every conscious thought led you to an action that progressed the relationship a little more, didn't it? The same must hold true for your idea.

At some point the entrepreneurs I've known and worked with have had to make a choice. Do they stay in their 9-to-5 jobs or do they commit themselves wholeheartedly to their new enterprises? Like

trying to juggle two romantic relationships at the same time, it's nigh on impossible to find fulfillment until you get to the stage where you are prepared to commit to just one. When it comes to your idea, you've got to do whatever it takes to commit yourself to it, just as much as you do when you find someone with whom you're in love.

4. Is there sufficient synergy between you and your idea to sustain a long-term relationship?

In Indian culture, it used to be common practice to review two people's horoscopes before declaring them a "match." In which case, we would look at the many attributes that defined each person to see how many points of commonality there were between them. Today, with Internet dating we do something similar, albeit more informally and less systematically. We read online profiles to check if we share similar hobbies and interests. Do we hold common values? Do we want the same things in life? Are our goals and objectives in alignment or not? Imagine that your idea is like a person to whom you plan to get married. Take this additional step to ask yourself if, as in the story I shared with you about my commitment to the online marketplace, the values that the potential business stands for and what you hold dear are one and the same. To be truly successful, you absolutely need to hold to the same vision.

Let me share one more brief example, concerning the founders of a startup called 4R Recycling, based in my hometown of Bangalore. They are in the business of recycling electronic waste and I'll be sharing more about their entrepreneurial efforts in Chapter Four.

While holding senior executive roles within major corporations, each of the three co-founders found they were contributing to the escalating sources of electronic waste, by which I mean the cell phones, laptops, desktops and the other technological tools we use in our lives, that become outdated every few years and are then cast aside when we buy the latest models. These co-founders decided to be part of the *solution* rather than continue contributing to the problem.

The CEO and Managing Director of 4R Recycling, Ramanathan N. had been the Chief Financial Officer of a multinational technology company where he was responsible for ensuring healthy gross margins every quarter. When he came to articulate for us the core theme that had to underpin his future business—even before he knew what that was—he said two things. One, he didn't want to be in a gross margins business, and two, he wanted to do something that was socially impactful. Both of which are true with respect to 4R Recycling. As such the two are a definite "match."

5. **If it came down to it, would you be prepared to live with this idea for the next 20 years of your life?**
As someone who has been happily married for more than twenty years, I can attest to the fact that the most successful marriages occur between two people who really like one another. For me and my wife, as well as all the friends who are similarly blessed, it is friendship that binds us together for the long haul.

When you think about your own long-term relationships, wouldn't you agree that what matters is *who* they are deep inside, not whether or not they are attractive, or smart, or make you laugh or whatever else surface characteristics most people care about? The same thing applies to your business. Every time you need a reason to support why you like your idea, that highlights a potential problem. As is the case with sustainable marriages, you need to address such problems head on rather than let them fester.

❋ ❋ ❋

I hope you have taken the time to answer these questions with reference to your ideas in an honest and unbiased way, and convinced yourself that at least one of them is a perfect fit for you. On the other hand, perhaps you have found that your answers still leave you with the sense that you're not quite ready to make that long-term commitment. In which case, it may be

worthwhile for you to take a step back and generate *more* ideas and check them against this orientation part of the FOUND process later.

However, if you feel your answers were satisfactory and your idea does orientate with your life, then you are pointed in the right direction in this ideation journey. As shown on our FOUND map, you are looking toward True North. I certainly encourage you to move forward with all such qualifying ideas.

❋ ❋ ❋

At this stage, I'm reminded me of the old saying, "The way ahead is the way to success." Which brings us neatly to the next step in the FOUND process. And that involves unearthing the research insights that will pay huge dividends to you in the long run.

Unearth

UNEARTH
Assumptions
© 2015 NAVEEN LAKKUR | ALL RIGHTS RESERVED

FOUND

I t is easy and indeed tempting to make assumptions about your ideas, especially when you are passionate about solving a funda-mental problem for society generally, within a specific market sector, or with a particular client or prospect need in mind.

Such unchecked assumptions, however, are likely to lead you down dead ends. Certainly, as far as proceeding with untenable ideas is concerned. That's because such expectations are often associated with what is known as "the curse of expertise." This is especially true if you are operating within a field or industry that you've been immersed in for some time.

I'll start by illustrating what I mean by "the curse of expertise" with a personal story, and then back up this contention with some scientific evidence.

Let me take you back thirty years, to a time when I was a young boy. The uncle of one of my closest friends took a group of us on an outing into the forest. We were young and excited and in exploratory mode as we ventured further and further into this natural environment. After a while, hot and tired from our exertions we came across a beautiful pond and were immediately excited at the thought of going for a long, cool swim.

One member of our group, another youth, was known as an expert swimmer. Upon seeing the water he immediately dove right in. What this boy didn't know was that the base of the pond was formed of quicksand, soft enough so that the dive didn't break his neck, but which still brought about his disastrous end. Our friend hit the bottom of the pond with such a force that his head got stuck far down into the quicksand and he was sucked in. He was unable to free himself—nor could we help him—and he died from asphyxiation. It was only with considerable effort and some creativity that we ended up pulling his body out of the pond at all.

The boy who died was considered an "expert" swimmer, yet his belief that he had enough know-how to keep himself safe in any body of water did him more harm than good on this occasion. In fact, it was this very assumption that got him killed. Similarly, when you begin your journey from idea to sustainable business you should think of yourself as entering unknown waters.

The more of an expert you are in your field, the more important it is for you to test your assumptions about your idea, rather than give way to them. In the case of the friend of mine who died, despite his confidence around water he would likely still be living today if, before taking that dive, he'd asked himself some important questions: How deep is the water? Might there be crocodiles or poisonous snakes lurking nearby? What other dangers am I not currently aware of? For the rest of us, the pond represented the same water and a beautiful opportunity to cool off after our long hike in the forest. Sadly for the swimming "expert," it became his final resting place.

The point of sharing this story with you is this: It is only by asking key questions and not assuming you know everything you need to know, that you're more likely to be successful in your endeavors. There is no guarantee you won't fail, of course, but through this step of researching and double-checking those things you take for granted, your chances of failure will reduce drastically. The responsibility for success or failure rests with you at this point.

Expertise: Help or Hindrance?

Now let me briefly share a study conducted a number of years ago by Stanford University professor, Pamela Hinds from the Department of Management Science and Engineering. She was interested in learning how experts conveyed information to novices and whether or not being an expert was a help or a hindrance in the sphere of cell phone technology[4].

Professor Hinds' study involved three different groups: First, the sales people who sold the cell phones and therefore were fully conversant with the technology. Second, those customers who had used the phones before and were merely upgrading. Third, the "novice" customers who had never used this particular technology before. Professor Hinds then asked the

---

4   Psychology Today, The Curse of Expertise, http://bit.ly/1NPy79x (accessed December 6, 2015)

sales people, representing the experts, to estimate how long they believed it would take someone not familiar with the technology and who had never owned that particular cell phone before, to become proficient in its use.

Now, you might expect that the experts—the sales people—would have had an appreciation of how well a novice would understand the written instructions offered as a guide to using the technology, within the overall package. And that they would have a clear understanding of the problems that these novice users of the technology faced, so they could guide them through their misconceptions and mistakes. Indeed, the expectation of these in-house experts was that the novices would find the instructions clear enough, such that someone new to the phone would need less than 13 minutes before being able to use it.

> *Those of us with expertise often don't fully understand the difficulties faced by people who don't share our expert knowledge and experience.*

That's not what Professor Hinds found, however. New customers took approximately 30 minutes, more than twice as long, before learning how to use the new phone. This just goes to show how those of us with expertise often don't fully understand the difficulties faced by people who don't share our expert knowledge and experience.

It is for these reasons that this next part of the FOUND process is so essential to you. You are going to discover two ways in which to validate the assumptions you may be holding about your idea and the market to which it applies:

1. With respect to the problem itself, it will help you become much more certain that the problem you believe you are solving is *actually* a problem that the market requires to be solved.
2. And, concerning the solution you are offering, it will help give you the confidence that you are building your business around the *best possible* solution.

Now let's look at two case study examples, one to illustrate each of these points.

Executing on the Right Problem

First, with respect to what is the realistically achievable problem that your idea and business intend to solve, let's look again at a company introduced in the last chapter, 4R Recycling. As you may remember, 4R's bigger vision is to become a complete end-to-end waste management company. Initially the founders believed that they could build their company such that they would convert *all* forms of waste into energy.

However, when they really began to research this issue, they discovered that this idea was not going to be economically viable. 4R operate out of Bangalore, India, one of the country's major metropolitan cities. One way in which Indian household waste differs from that generated in the West is that a huge amount of waste is what is called "wet waste." Most Indian families still cook their meals "from scratch," using fresh vegetables, fruits and other high water-content products. In order to utilize waste that can be effectively converted into energy, this waste would first have to be dried out, which reduces the amount of waste available for conversion by around 30 per cent.

Why was that a problem? Because 4R would still have had to pay for the tonnage of the original "wet" waste, rather than the weight of the waste that they would be able to utilize. In other words, they would be paying 30 per cent more for the waste they could effectively recycle, quite aside from the time and effort involved to transform it into useful waste.

It was at this point that 4R's research set them on a much more economically viable path: that of electronic waste. They knew from what they had read online and in various reports that electronics consumption in India represented a USD $400 billion market, and this market was only going to grow. (Indeed, as pointed out in the previous chapter, the co-founders had experienced—as executives in major corporations—just what a voracious appetite companies, universities and schools, non-profits and other charitable organizations have for technological devices.)

The other plus point about focusing on the e-waste problem, rather than embracing the broader waste management issue, was that this was a sun-raising idea, rather than a sun-setting one. What do I mean by that?

> While you are engaging in your research, it is important to determine whether the problem you plan to address is one that is growing rather than diminishing.

While you are engaging in your research, it is important to determine whether the problem you plan to address is one that is growing rather than diminishing. In 4R's case, all trends pointed to increased consumption of electronic goods, while at the same time the lifespan of such devices was decreasing. That is, consumers were replacing their existing technology at a faster rate. Looked at from that perspective, 4R's co-founders were confident that by focusing on electronic waste, their company had a rosy future, one that was also "recession proof."

Had 4R held to the assumption that an end-to-end waste management solution was right for their company, the chances are that they would have run out of money before too long. As it was, a deep understanding of the context of their market (the "wet waste" issue inherent in India), and being flexible enough to hold to their bigger vision without expecting to be able to realize it in the short or even medium term, was what enabled 4R to create a stronger foothold in the niche arena of electronic waste recycling.

Building the Best Solution

For the second point—unearthing the evidence that will ensure you focus on the best possible solution for the problem you are tackling—let's look at another entrepreneurial venture out of India. Remember Autowale, the Pune-based company mentioned in Chapter Two, that developed predictive software to help connect autorickshaw drivers with customers?

When they originally conceived their idea, Autowale's founders Janardan Prasad and Mukesh Jha were excited about what technology could best facilitate this connection. One of their early assumptions was that they could track the drivers using a GPS device, either through a cell phone or one that was separately installed within the vehicle, similar to the way taxi companies operate. However, it was only when Janardan and Mukesh drove around with some of the drivers and spoke with them face-to-face, did they become fully aware of the specific challenges associated with this form of transportation.

First, they found during their pilot study that using GPS drains the battery of cell phones very quickly. Since the vast majority of auto rickshaws don't have a charging point within the vehicle, it would present difficulties for them trying to keep those cell phone sufficiently charged. Another feature of auto rickshaws is that they are open sided and so security is always an issue. Even assuming a GPS device could be installed within the vehicle, there was a high probability that it would be stolen. Plus, there would be the logistics issues of having to regularly service such devices.

There was one other contextual consideration as to why supplying their auto rickshaw drivers with GPS-installed cell phones was going to be a problem. As Autowale's founders discovered through talking with these drivers, as well the unions that represented them, the vast majority of the men are poorly educated. Most of these drivers typically only know how to use two buttons: the green one for connecting a call, and the red one that ends the call. Therefore it wasn't going to be practical to supply drivers with a Smartphone and expect them, without considerable education and training, to learn how to use the GPS facility.

Many entrepreneurs might have become disillusioned at this point and wondered if they were ever going to solve the problem of how best to link a specific auto rickshaw driver's route with a booking customer. Janardan and Mukesh, however, saw this as an opportunity to revise their business model, in a way that differentiated them even more, and hence gave them a greater competitive edge.

As Janardan explains: "Because none of the things we had originally thought about were going to work, this gave rise to a more innovative approach—one that no one else in India was doing, because the usual way was to rely on a hardware device. We realized we had to do things

differently and that led us to write our proprietary software in which we *predict* the location of our drivers using a lot of different data.

"We also modified our business model so that instead of saying to customers, "Call us now and we'll send you a rickshaw in five minutes," we asked that they give us some advance notice to take traffic and other delays into account. The driver will arrive on time and will handle the trip in an efficient, professional manner, but we need some time to arrange that. The moment we started doing that, we found that our customers were happy to book the ride an hour or more in advance."

Learning from Failures and Successes

Bear in mind that at this point of the Unearth stage you are only determining the *need* for your idea or solution. I am talking about the research you have to conduct that will prepare you for the next step, which is taking the action based on this new knowledge and understanding. Essentially what you are training yourself to do is to get into the right mindset for sustainable success, one in which you don't make the potentially costly and time-wasting mistake of assuming that what you believe to be true *is* true! You are still at the point at which you are *confirming* that your idea has legs.

> What we have to do is to learn from others' mistakes as well as their successes.

I remember the time I was meeting with my boss and mentor, who asked me an interesting question: "Naveen, do you think we should learn from our mistakes?" My response was presumably the same one that you would have given: Absolutely!

He then went on to ask: "Do we have enough time to do that all by ourselves?" At which point I had to agree that we did not. What we have to do is to learn from others' mistakes as well as their successes.

As Dr. Liz Alexander and I went about interviewing many highly successful entrepreneurs for this book, one of several patterns emerged. Each of our interviewees was a highly curious individual who had unearthed information from many sources. Ajay Goel, the venture capitalist you will be introduced to in more depth in Chapter Seven, for example, loves reading autobiographies. These real life stories provide him with considerable understanding of how prominent people in different industries and with different life experiences to himself have created value in the world.

As you explore similar stories yourself—from books, as part of case studies, or as articles in business magazines or academic journals—you should use the opportunity to explore why some ideas failed while others succeeded. Perhaps failure was merely a timing issue. Maybe the idea was ahead of its time and so the people who would have benefited from it were not able to relate to it or understand its value (for which see the example of Ask Me on page 78). Or it may have been that the inventor or entrepreneur needed to engage in a certain amount of further education and was not willing or able to do that successfully.

Similarly, you should analyze what contributed to someone's success, such as personal characteristics (i.e., their orientation to their idea), the market trends at the time, or the specific actions they took.

As I hope you will appreciate from the stories shared earlier about 4R Recycling and Autowale, while conducting "desk" research on your computer can be an invaluable way to set the direction for further unearthing, the most meaningful and real information will always come from getting out into the field.

Of course, given that entrepreneurs are highly action-oriented individuals, many of us feel that spending time and effort in conducting research isn't speaking to our strengths, or even that it is a waste to time. Should you remain unconvinced that the Unearth stage of the FOUND process is essential to your future success, here are two further brief examples to consider.

Failure as a Stepping Stone to Success

This first story is one I was exposed to while listening to V.S.S. Mani, the founder and CEO of JustDial, when he was speaking at a conference in Mumbai. Mani is also featured in the *Young Turks* book mentioned previously (see Chapter Two).

FOUND

In 1989, a young and ambitious Mani, together with two business partners, decided to launch Ask Me. They conceived this as disrupting the monopoly of Yellow Pages before the Age of the Internet, by producing a 24/7 phone-in service that did away with the need to publish local service directories. After struggling for a year and a half they realized that there was not enough money to continue running the business. What did this failure have to do with a lack of research? Well, although the idea appeared sound, it turned out not to be aligned with market demand. For one thing, in those days there were only four million phone connections among an Indian population of 800 million. As Mani himself explains in *Young Turks:* "Telecom itself was so under-penetrated, that reaching out to the prospective user was a big challenge. Even if we had got funding, the lack of ecosystem would have meant we would have still struggled for a long, long time."

In Mani's words, "We were perhaps too young and didn't know how to run a business."

I'm not sure about the "too young" part, given the age of the many successful young entrepreneurs I mentor these days. But one way you can demonstrate that you are mature enough to run a business is by conducting sufficient research to validate your ideas, before spending too much money.

In Mani's case, he took this "failed" experience and leveraged it into his latest venture, JustDial, a call-in service that customers can use to find just about any product or service they are looking for. This was an idea that Mani could grow into a large enterprise, which is now listed on both the National Stock Exchange of India (NSE) and the Bombay Stock Exchange (BSE).

* * *

For one female entrepreneur who went through the Founder Institute program in Bangalore, however, her research meant she had no option but to walk away from her "winning" idea.

Failing Quickly: A Boon, not a Jinx

This aspiring entrepreneur had already worked for over 10 years in several large telecom companies and was very passionate about her telecom-related idea. She believed that her solution would help large telecom companies provide a better customer care service to their entire user base.

By the time she got to this phase, this entrepreneur—let's call her Sujata—had already brought on board two people to help her build programs, and she already had one potential large brand customer. It was only at this point, being guided to engage in some preliminary market research, that Sujata found out that another technologist in the U.S. already held patents for the approach she intended to take. It became clear that if she had carried on this path and her business had become successful, the patent holder would have come after her and sued.

Typically, we find that if an idea is not successful and has no value, the entrepreneur needs to drop it. But in Sujata's case, it was because she didn't own the intellectual property (IP) for the concept. There was every indication she could have built a hugely successful business based on her idea, the trouble was that someone had got there first and had already patented the concept.

Luckily for her, the cost of failure was still low. Through unearthing this potential problem, Sujata was able to pull the plug within the fifth week of embarking on the Founder Institute course, rather than finding herself five years down the road embroiled in costly litigation. She was happy to let go of the idea and is now in the process of developing and validating some new ideas so that she can re-embark on her entrepreneurial journey.

❈ ❈ ❈

In these kinds of examples, it calls for a celebration if you fail early enough. Because it means that you have saved yourself from wasting all those precious resources such as time, effort and money. This is the phase that has

the power to change the dynamics of your business, or the future course of your business. If you can alert yourself quickly to the not-so-obvious, and understand and appreciate what your research is telling you, then without doubt you will experience some of the remarkable 'aha' moments that inevitably follow.

> This is the phase that has the power to change the dynamics of your business, or the future course of your business.

For example, one personal 'aha' moment came about when I was conducting the research for this book. While interviewing the many successful founders whose stories we have captured and shared that relate to their journeys from idea stage to successful business, we found there were many common themes. But the one that hit me most was that although each of these entrepreneurs reached that milestone we like to call "success," it was *never* their original idea that got them there. Because in every single one of these cases, their original ideas had morphed into something quite different by the time they achieved that success.

I strongly urge you to use this opportunity to ask yourself the tough questions that the Unearth part of the FOUND process requires. Because you can be sure that your prospective investors will do so even if you don't, and it's wise to have an answer ready. For example, investigate whether anyone else has attempted the same approach as the one you are intending to develop. Find out who might have explored this idea and failed, then try and uncover exactly why it was that they did not succeed. Conversely, has anyone succeeded with the same or similar idea? Even go back to basics and ask yourself and others, whether there is an actual need for this solution you propose, one that people value enough that they will willingly pay for it.

What you will discover while engaging in such "unearthing" are the gems you'll need in order to confidently enter the next phase in our journey, which I call "negotiation." Because as much as I know that entrepreneurs love to create, rather than spend what can often be seen as "wasted time" thinking and researching, this investment will pay dividends in the weeks and months to come.

So, are you ready to hear more about the next phase? Then, please, let's continue the journey.

Negotiate

Not too long ago I was approached by a former executive with an extremely impressive resumé, who had once worked for a large global technology company. This man had come up with a new idea and was going through the FOUND process in order to increase his chances of turning it into a viable and sustainable business. He wanted to give me an update, as he now planned to launch this idea into the world fairly soon. We met over dinner and close to the end of our discussion he said to me, "This is all confidential of course, Naveen, so please keep what I've told you to yourself." I agreed that I would, given his apparent nervousness, although what I really wanted to ask him was *why*. But then, I suspected I already knew the answer. He was afraid that his idea would be stolen by someone else.

Have you ever felt the same way about an idea of your own? Indeed, have you ever talked with a trusted advisor, only to ask them to keep the information confidential? Many entrepreneurs do this, but it is not the best course of action. What this man should have said to me, given how highly networked I am and how he was all set to launch his business in any case, was whether I would be willing to talk to 100 of my contacts about his plan, in order to garner some interest and possibly even locate a client or two. As it was, because I had promised not to say anything, no one in my circle was able to know or contribute to the idea.

> Most entrepreneurs don't realize how difficult it is to secure those first few clients or customers.

Most entrepreneurs don't realize how difficult it is to secure those first few clients or customers. But if you can crack that challenge early on, your business will likely go from strength to strength. Why? Because most people adhere to what's called "social proof." This refers to the influence that comes from prospective clients and customers seeing that others are already doing business with you. These prospects then make assumptions about the success of your business, based on the fact that you are already selling to your market, and the wisdom of following suit. In other words, having someone who is already buying what you have to offer makes it much more likely that others will do likewise.

The Importance of Early Customers

This chapter is all about getting those first few early customers. And there's no need to worry if you don't feel you are entirely ready to produce the goods. Big organizations like Oracle and Microsoft have always been strategic in this way, sending their sales people out with just the glimmer of an idea to see if anyone bites. Then, when they do, that gives everyone in the company the green light to go ahead and build something, even if it means telling those first clients that implementation is going to take several more months.

I previously used the analogy of dating and considering marriage to emphasize how important it is to orientate your idea to who you are and what you value. Now I'm going to talk about the relationship you have with your idea as if it were *already* a marriage. Because, let's face it, you can make all the assumptions you want about a person but it's not until you experience them day in, day out that you can really see whether the qualities you expected them to have are for real.

Similarly, when it comes to the process of ideation, you will only really know whether what you have to offer is what people want, not only by going out and talking to them, but by asking them to commit to you. In this phase you are not just validating your idea, you're also fine tuning it.

Let me share another story to illustrate what I mean by that.

The "Winning Idea" That Wasn't

As a mentor for the Founder Institute in Bangalore I once worked with a man with years of experience in the field of human resources (HR), who aspired to become an entrepreneur. As part of our work together I took him through the FOUND methodology and, as you will shortly discover, saved him considerable wasted time, money and effort.

One of the strengths this man felt he had was in understanding the importance of relationships in business. His idea was to create something he called "Experience Zones" within organizations. In the same way that Starbucks would have a presence within a university campus, for example, he wanted to do the same thing focused on selling high quality cookies,

chocolates and ice cream for large organizations. His thinking was that if organizations provided this kind of service for their employees it would boost employee engagement, which had become a hot topic in the business world.

When we met, this HR executive had already devised a plan. He told me that he knew the HR field and was very clear on why he believed there was a need for such an experience. Having reached this phase of the FOUND process I urged him to go out and talk with his fellow HR professionals to ensure that he had sufficient corporate backing. This seemed as if it would pose no problem for him at all, since he had already visited 25 different companies and had been told by everyone he met that this was a brilliant idea and he should go ahead and launch these Experience Zones.

> Not one person who had praised the idea when he had mentioned it to them would sign on.

But the point about the Negotiation phase is that people's tacit agreement is not enough. The HR executive's assignment at this stage was to get at least three letters of intent, because while it was gratifying to have all that verbal support for his idea, I knew it would be unwise for him to move forward unless he already had several written commitments from these supporters.

How many letters of intent do you think this man was able to achieve, having already visited 25 enthusiastic companies?

The answer is: None! Not one person who had praised the idea when he had mentioned it to them would sign on. In short, they were not prepared to put their money where their mouths were. As such, all that enthusiasm meant nothing. My mentee was never able to convince his contacts to truly buy into his idea by making an actual financial investment.

Why do you think that was?

I believe it was because his idea was a "nice to have," but not a "need to have." Indeed, although the HR executive talked a good talk about employee engagement, and had all this long-standing experience, he had never been able to articulate the value to potential clients in any tangible way. For example, he had no evidence that this kind of on-site service would boost retention and employee engagement as he had suggested it would, which are issues that are especially important in high churn industries. He wasn't solving a serious problem, in contrast to Rajeev Pathak whom you will read about in the next chapter, and who was successful in transforming research connections into paying customers.

Can you see why this exercise was so valuable to the HR expert I just mentioned? There was a huge advantage to him in *failing* at this stage, rather than building such a marketplace and then finding no one was prepared to pay him for it.

Remember, many business people—especially those you already consider to be your friends and supporters, or who have known you in a professional capacity for some time, will want to wave you on to entrepreneurial success. Likewise, for this HR executive, everyone wanted to sound encouraging and avoid squashing his enthusiasm. But when it came to doing business, it was very easy for these supposed supporters to say no because they were not convinced of a tangible return on their investment. Ignorance is not bliss when you are serious about your business.

So, this is the step in the FOUND process where the rubber meets the road, you might say. And it's a critical step, because without attracting tangible support for your business idea by persuading at least three people to sign letters of intent, you may end up creating a solution that is still looking for a problem.

Defining "Negotiation"

This is where my own definition of negotiation might come in useful. When most people think of negotiating they believe this always implies money, but that's not necessarily true. What you are looking to do here is achieve valid commitments by creating a win:win for both sides. It may be that one or more of the three interested parties—meaning those who have committed by signing on the dotted line—will endorse or collaborate with you without any money necessarily changing hands.

For example, let's say one of your interested parties is a key influencer within a networking organization, that could be very good for your business going forward. You may agree to pilot your solution with them at no cost, in exchange for publicly associating their name with your product or service.

Alternatively, you could offer these early supporters a discounted solution in exchange for committing to your business for an extended period of time—say, lower prices for three years' worth of visibility. You may need to be creative when it comes to working with these early adopters, so that both sides get what they need from the collaboration.

Surveying your prospects

For consumer-facing businesses it is vital that this negotiation stage involves surveying a large number of people—ideally around 500 if possible. The good news is, this is so much easier, cheaper and faster these days with the availability of some simple online survey tools. These tools will not only allow you to define your survey questions, comprising of both close-ended and open-ended responses, but will create a link for you that recipients can use to directly access the survey online.

The following are some recommended resources that include both free and premium (paid) options:

- SurveyMonkey (**www.surveymonkey.com**)
- Zoomerang (**www.zoomerang.com**)
- SoGoSurvey (**www.sogosurvey.com**)
- PollDaddy (**www.polldaddy.com**)
- SurveyPlanet (**https://www.surveyplanet.com**)
- FormSite (**www.formsite.com**)
- KwikSurveys (**https://kwiksurveys.com**)
- SurveyGizmo (**www.surveygizmo.com**)
- ConstantContact (**www.constantcontact.com**)
- QuestionPro (**www.questionpro.com**)

Crowdsource Your Way to Success

Another way to gather opinions about your business idea might come from the trend for crowdsourcing. For example, in the city in which I live an initiative called NextBangalore is being promoted to entice citizens and other stakeholders (businesses, government, non-profit organizations and others), to suggest and debate ideas for how Bangalore can change to meet current and future needs.

In the U.S.A., a senator used an online program called Madison 2.0 to crowdsource ideas for the OPEN Act, protecting Internet freedom and intellectual property online. And on the tiny island of Guernsey, which lies in the English Channel between the U.K. and France, residents have used crowdsourcing tools including Google Docs and Google Moderator to gather ideas that would inform legislation concerning the use of Google's driverless cars on the island.

Similarly, think about how you might use surveys and crowdsourcing to further strengthen, as well as promote, your business idea.

While this phase helps you ground your ideas, you will hopefully see that it could also help to set the direction for your business and maybe even build its initial momentum.

* * *

Now that I have addressed the negotiation stage, you are ready to enter what many consider to be the most difficult phase of ideation. That is, to decide or determine which ideas to discard in favor of "the winner." For which we can learn from others who have done precisely that—coming next.

Determine or Decide

How do you choose a single idea when you have so many wonderful opportunities tugging at you for attention? At this point you might feel it would be an almost impossible choice to select one idea that you can transform into a sustainable business, without regretting that decision. That's because it's hard to let go of our "darlings," whether they be one or more good ideas, or a wonderful paragraph we may have written for a book.

The good news is that by following the FOUND process, that choice will be easier than you think. My experience has taught me that if you thoroughly orientate each idea against what you stand for and who you are, unearth all that invaluable research, and enter into negotiations with interested parties before going too far forward, the right idea will rise to the top.

To illustrate this, let me tell you what happened when a close friend of mine applied to 15 universities in the U.S. to enter into the Ph.D. program of a very specific course she was interested in. The good news was that she was accepted into 14 of those schools, including Harvard. Nevertheless, my friend selected a university in Atlanta, Georgia. So, how and why did she make that particular choice?

One of her reasons for choosing the Atlanta college was because of her focus on the reputation of the faculty within that particular department, and her desire to work with renowned individuals in their field. It wasn't the name of the overall university that was important to her, hence her decision not to choose a famous university like Harvard, but the actual department and faculty with which she would be forever associated.

The second reason concerned money. As you may already be aware, the cost of a graduate education can be crippling to a young person and it can take many years, if not decades, to repay those loans. In order to attend a college like Harvard, for example, my friend would have had to take out a loan or borrow from her father, neither of which she was prepared to do. In contrast, the Atlanta college offered her a generous monthly stipend that took care of all her expenses and meant that she would be able to complete the Ph.D. program with no ongoing debt. At the end of the day, that was much more important to her.

Can you see how being clear about her values and motivations (as in the Orientate step), and researching the various courses (Unearth), made it easy for my friend to reject those other 13 universities out of the 14 who had offered her a place? Similarly, you will have your own methodology for choosing which idea you want to pursue.

As in the case of my friend, your criteria may be something no one else can understand. Some people felt she was crazy not to go to Harvard, but my friend was the expert in knowing herself and what she wanted to accomplish and therefore was the better judge. Taking on a major commitment like a Ph.D. or founding a business—unless it is done by yourself, for yourself—will undoubtedly end up feeling less pleasurable and satisfying.

The same thing is true at this stage when you are deciding on which is your winning idea. By using the personalized yet rigorous FOUND methodology outlined in this book, the criteria you will set out for yourself will make it much easier to make that final determination.

There are two parts to this. The first is the choice you make to move forward with that one idea, and the second is your decision to let go or "kill off" all your other ideas. (You may be interested to know that the suffix *cide* as in decide, homicide, and pesticide comes from the Latin meaning "killer" or "the act of killing.")

CASE STUDY: RAJEEV PATHAK, eDream Edusoft & 'funtoot'

Founded in 2010 and headquartered in Bangalore, India, eDream Edusoft has invented the world's first intelligent and adaptive personal tutor for K-12 students. This remarkably fun, web-based product (offering a curriculum currently in science and math), is called 'funtoot.' Blending the company's innovative software algorithms with outstanding pedagogical understanding from renowned educational experts, 'funtoot' provides that all-important one-on-one attention, encouragement and automated tutoring that is known to facilitate each child's innate genius.

 FOUND

Instead of requiring children to adapt to the educational environment, ignoring their individual and unique interests, abilities, and attention spans as traditional school-based education is largely set up to do, 'funtoot' adapts itself to each child's needs. In addition to being used in schools across India, the company is launching 'funtoot' in Southeast Asia and the Middle East, and is running one pilot project within schools in the Bay Area of California.

I got to know the founder and CEO, Rajeev Pathak, through the Founder Institute in Bangalore, where we are both mentors. You may already be familiar with Rajeev if you have seen or read about the Bloomberg UTV reality series *Pitch, Season 2* and know that he was the final winner from among 400 original entrepreneurs that had all been vying for the 5 crore (then worth USD \$1 million) investment, which was the show's "prize." In talking with Rajeev about how he transformed this particular idea into a growing business, it was obvious that he had unconsciously used the same principles that you are being introduced to, through the FOUND methodology.

This particular case study serves two purposes:

1. To demonstrate how easy it can be to reject or "kill off" other good ideas, because of what you learn through the earlier steps.
2. To confirm that one idea above all will become the *only* idea you would want to develop.

While you might expect me to jump immediately to the idea de-selection process, this will not make sense without setting some context for why, out of all the educationally focused ideas that he could have proceeded with, Rajeev Pathak elected to develop 'funtoot.' For which we need to go back to when he was a boy, brought up in the countryside of northern India.

Rajeev's Story

As remarkable as it may appear now, when talking about a man with a master's degree in Business Administration from IIM Bangalore and an M.Tech from BITS Pilani (the same institution as the redBus founders, mentioned in Chapter Two), and who has won many awards during the time he worked for Wipro, Rajeev did not have a conventional schooling until he was 10 years old. Instead, he was home schooled by his grandfather, which meant he got individualized attention with a greater emphasis on life skills and a strong value system than he would have done learning by "rote". It wasn't until Rajeev's mother pushed for her son to go to school with other children of his age that he was sent to a government primary school, some miles away from where he lived.

That school only offered a 5th grade education, so a year later Rajeev moved even further away from his home to stay with an uncle, also a teacher, so that he could attend junior and middle school. At the age of 10, Rajeev learned a great deal about independence by returning home on his own with multiple stops in order to change buses, having to do his work by himself at uncle's place, and needing to discipline himself enough to complete his homework without parental supervision. It was during this time that Rajeev also learned what is known as "delayed gratification," because he couldn't just help himself to whatever he wanted, given that he was living in someone else's home.

From the ages of 10 through 17, Rajeev—transitioning yet again to another uncle's home to complete his high school education—experienced many things that required him to embrace the new, take risks, and rise above adversity. All of which perfectly prepared him to become a start-up entrepreneur later in his career.

It was during the time he worked for Wipro Technologies as a software engineer, having excelled in his own education, that Rajeev helped build a USD $100 million software business with global customers. Through this experience, he became sure that world class products could be developed in India. A confluence of events led to his realization that something needed to be done in the realm of early education, one of which was having children of his own and noticing that schools were not self-sufficient places for learning. This experience reinforced his belief that if you make an impact on learning at a young age this is considerably easier to bring about than waiting until the student is in high school or college, and has lasting value.

No Shortage of Ideas

Other than a desire to do something in the field of education, Rajeev moved ahead with a clean slate and an open mind. Several ideas had come to him, but he also realized that while his technology and business backgrounds were valuable, he knew little or nothing about education. His original ideas were to:

- Build some kind of educational tool or learning device that children could use.
- Develop a collaborative platform that would help bridge the gap between students, teachers, and parents.
- Create ebooks with an educational slant.
- Produce a diagnostics tool to analyze a child's learning orientations and preferences.
- Build an educational marketplace where anyone could create educational content that was shareable with a broader audience.

As you can see, Rajeev had no shortage of ideas, so on the face of it he appeared to be in a strong position as far as the free-flow step of the FOUND methodology is concerned. And, of course, given his own background he had already established a strong connection or "orientation" between his own life experience and that of the company he hoped to build.

But then came the need to "unearth"—to conduct the research that would help validate one of those ideas. And it was at this point that everything changed.

With the realization that he was not an expert in school education, Rajeev visited dozens of different schools, speaking with teachers, school administrators and parents in order to get a clearer sense of the most fundamental problems they faced. At schools where there were 50 kids in a class, he heard how teachers struggled to give each child individual attention. In schools where they had 20 kids in each class he heard the same thing. They would have loved to offer students one-on-one personalized attention and tutoring, but this just wasn't feasible. Even in schools with an enviable ratio of one teacher for every 10 students, the message was the same. The solution to bringing out each child's innate potential was to work with them one-on-one. And this issue clearly resonated with Rajeev as he'd had the benefit of being taught this way by his grandfather when he was a young boy himself.

There appeared to be no immediate solution to this fundamental problem, however. After all, it just wasn't practical or economically viable to have so many human beings working exclusively with individual children. But Rajeev believed that technology could provide an answer.

Before we move forward with that thought, let's revisit a challenge mentioned earlier in Chapter Five, that of building a solution than having to look for a problem that it would fit. It became patently obvious to Rajeev that none of the five ideas he'd been playing around with *before* conducting this market research were of interest to the market he aimed to serve. With some of them, like producing a learning device or creating ebooks, there were many other players in the same market. This was no way to create a *differentiated* product and company.

Changing the World, One Idea at a Time

When we look again at Rajeev's personal orientation, this is a man who loves to grapple with *enormous* challenges. His interest lay in solving a problem with a huge and profound impact. In other words, in his own way and like so many other hugely successful and fulfilled entrepreneurs, Rajeev wanted to change the world.

The value of having conducted this rigorous market research—not just by visiting a handful of schools, but by cross-checking what he discovered in dozens of different institutions—and by knowing himself and what was important to him personally, was that Rajeev found it easy to eliminate those other ideas. The big idea on which his company would be built had to create enormous value and directly impact learning. In his own words: "The other ideas could have solved some problem but our impact would not have been as great, because other companies could do the same thing."

So far we have addressed—through Rajeev's case study—the F (free-flow of ideas), the O (orientation of the individual with the idea), and the U (the unearthing of research that can help validate one idea above all). Now we come to the N or negotiation part of the process.

> The other ideas could have solved some problem but our impact would not have been as great, because other companies could do the same thing.

Because he had made so many connections within the dozens of schools that engaged with him in his research phase, it was easy for Rajeev to then partner with 12 of those schools. They not only became the company's prototype customers but, in a co-creation capacity, helped in the development and further validation of the 'funtoot' product.

Can you see how valuable this was to Rajeev's fledgling company? When eDream Edusoft began building 'funtoot,' there was no question in their mind that there was a huge market need. It wasn't a case of creating a product based on their own assumptions, and then trying to sell that on. Plus, when you are trying to sell an innovative idea to new customers, they are going to feel much more confident in knowing that people *just like them* have not only endorsed the product or service, but had a hand in its creation.

Today, eDream Edusoft is living the dream of its founder in solving a fundamental problem inherent in the current classroom setup. 'Funtoot' is helping to bring out the innate talents of 50,000 school students from the ages of 7 and 15 in math and science—and that figure is continuously rising.

The solution also adds value in supporting teachers who, in a perfect world, would love to teach only one child at a time—listening to, adapting to, and appropriately guiding that young mind in a way that is personalized and powerful.

To learn more about 'funtoot' and the company's successes, go to **www.funtoot.com**. Then ask yourself this question: What is the biggest takeaway for you from Rajeev Pathak's inspiring story? And how much can you use that understanding to decide which of your ideas might take you forward to similar success?

* * *

Speaking of moving forward, let's now consider another facet of the entrepreneurial journey that so often is ignored or overlooked. One that involves understanding at the outset in which category your idea "fits," and at what market stage.

Chapter Seven

Navigating the Matrix

As we have all heard many times before, and I've expressed continually through this book, ideas are a dime a dozen. That's because the human mind is such a wonderful workshop and our ingenuity so innate that there is unlimited potential to generate ideas. But that's only a small part of what will ensure your entrepreneurial success.

I trust that having read and acted upon the FOUND process outlined in the previous chapters, you are now in a position to execute on an idea for which there is a sizeable market. One that is ready to pay for the service or product you are offering, in exchange for solving a problem that they haven't been able to address elsewhere up to now. Of course, that's easier said than done! Anyone can predict that we will one day colonize Mars, as science fiction writers are fond of suggesting, or create machines whose conversation and intellect cannot be distinguished from that of humans. But we all know that what fires our imaginations can be extremely challenging to deliver. I believe it is the combination of the idea *and* its execution that makes for the most powerful, winning solutions. Which is why, up to this point in the book, I have talked a lot about ideas and, to a certain extent, about execution.

There is, however, another message that I alluded to at the beginning of this book that I want to re-examine here. And that is that not all ideas can, or should, become businesses. This was part of the message I gave to

Sunil when he came to me with his TV gadget idea. Every entrepreneur has to learn the art of picking the *right* idea so that they increase their chances of developing it into a successful, sustainable business.

As I pointed out in the Introduction to this book, no idea is a bad idea as long we know how to categorize it and take the appropriate action. After all, expectations and actions are two very different things. We can't expect an idea to make us wealthy and create employment and perhaps satisfy a global market, if we treat it as a hobby. And if the idea is only worthy of remaining a hobby or side interest, then it would be foolish to waste our time and money trying to make it otherwise. This is where an understanding of different *categories* of ideas, together with the specific market stages into which they fit, will make a big difference to you going forward.

Indeed, both of these points are covered in this chapter. You want to be able to create a new strategy and an appropriate plan of action for executing your idea in order to make it into a successful reality. In which case, there needs to be some method for what might seem like chaotic madness at the moment. As I just pointed out, this involves understanding that there are different classifications of ideas, based on the category into which they fit, or the market stage.

Let me explain what I mean by both "category" and "market stage."

Categories and Markets

First, let's look at the categories, which you can see listed down the left hand column of the 6 x 6 matrix shown in Figure 1, and which I'll explain briefly next:

Figure 1

IDEA MATRIX

<---------------------- MARKET STAGE ---------------------->

IDEAS	YESTER YEAR	DECLINING	IN DEMAND	EARLY STAGE	GREEN FIELD	UNKNOWN
ENTREPRENERUAL						
INTRAPRENEURIAL						
PRODUCT						
PATENT						
PLUG-IN						
PASS-TIME						

<----------------------- CATEGORY ----------------------->

- **Entrepreneurial ideas**: These are the ideas that have the potential to sustain and grow, such that an organization can be built around them. The risk factor is obviously much higher in the entrepreneurial journey, but then you are trading high risk for high reward. Having said that, this book shows you the way to ground such ideas strongly, even as you aspire to reach the stars.

- **Intrapreneurial ideas:** These ideas are typically centered around the core technology of an existing organization and can perhaps be developed into initiatives with the potential to become separate business units within the corporate environment. While there's no change in the process to be followed for ideation in an intrapreneurial journey, the key sponsor for the initiative in this case will be the corporate entity you work for.

- **Product**: An idea that is higher up the value chain because it can be monetized and replicated with consistency.

- **Patent**: Receiving a patent recognizes and distinguishes ideas that are new and novel, like the coffee sleeve mentioned in an earlier chapter. By completing the necessary paperwork and following the correct procedures, the idea may receive a patent, which allows the inventor of the idea to claim ownership. As a matter of fact, it is a source of pride to be in this club, and you can find annual lists that show which countries and companies have registered the most patents globally[5].

- **Plug-in**: This refers to a feature or functionality that fits within an existing system or a product, such as Sunil's TV remote gadget discussed in the Introduction and Chapter One.

- **Pastime**: Anything that stems from a hobby or an activity you do "on the side," as opposed to thinking it will become a business (see also the reference to Facebook on page 81).

---

5   For example, World Intellectual Property Organization (WIPO): http://bit.ly/1HOMRTJ

However, in addition to the above-mentioned categories, it is important to understand the other dimension of the idea landscape that can help you determine which stage, in terms of the timescale, into which your idea fits. Look along the horizontal column of the matrix (Figure 1 on page 77) and you will see the names of the market stages. Again, here are some short descriptions of each:

- **Yesteryear**: This stage means that the relevance of the idea is stronger in the past than it is today. So, for example, let's say you have the idea of building a nice new feature for pagers that produces a different color back-lit glow to indicate the emotion of the message being received. While the idea of color indication based on message "mood" seems new and novel and may be patentable (as long as it's not already owned by someone else, of course), the pager technology itself is considered old-fashioned. While this stage may speak to "old" technologies, however, don't assume that a fresh idea cannot reinvigorate them, as was the case for Brompton Bike Hire (see page 28), when they originally introduced the folding, portable bicycle and collaborated with transportation authorities to make this "green" option available to commuters in the U.K. The same is true of turntables that play vinyl records, which have attracted a niche market among some music lovers.
- **Declining**: This refers to low demand or "sun setting," markets such as those that currently exist for things like fax machines and land-line telephones. Although, again, with the right twist even these ideas can be given a new lease of life, since there is still some market and people wanting to buy.
- **In-Demand**: In such a market there are great opportunities for "sun raising" ideas, such as building an interesting app for a touch screen Smartphone, which are in demand now all around the world, rather than trying to create a new waterproof jacket for a key-pad regular phone whose market share is declining.

- **Early Stage**: This stage of the market is where entrepreneurial ideas mushroom, but also tends to be where a lot of me-too ideas emerge. For example, as the Internet Age is maturing and the adoption of mobile technology is catching on, we are seeing many existing and new businesses and ideas shifting their solutions onto mobile, in the form of apps. And this is just the beginning, as there will likely be millions more new apps in the weeks, months, and years to come.

- **Green Field**: This relates to ideas that are so innovative there is no current market for them—you have to create one, perhaps within a larger market space. These ideas are often referred to as "radical innovation" and have the potential to disrupt an existing market. One example of this is WiTricity Corporation[6], whose wireless energy solution and patented technology aims to deliver power directly to devices such as computers and cell phones, without the need for access to a direct power source. WiTricity's technology, which has applications across many different markets, will eliminate the need to have access to wall sockets, to carry around bulky cables, and addresses the inconvenience and waste of continually replacing disposable batteries.

- **Unknown**: There is a thin line between the previous Green Field category and this particular market category. You can't hold ideas in this 'unknown' or unexplored market stage for very long. Indeed, the idea itself may be more suited to a pastime or a science fiction novel. For example, when President John F. Kennedy spoke about landing a man on the Moon and returning him safely to Earth, that sounded like wishful thinking at the time. Nevertheless a lot of amazing products have emerged from the efforts of NASA to make that dream a reality.

---

6   See: http://bit.ly/1PMvBRH

Building a Hobby

At this point you might be wondering what you should do about a "hobby" or pastime idea. Sadly, on many occasions aspiring entrepreneurs have tried to fit such ideas into the entrepreneurial journey and found that, despite their expectations and enormous efforts, they have yielded minimal or no results. That tends to be the case most of the time in this category. However, even though your expectations of transforming a hobby or pastime idea into a business are not great, you might find that it has the power to switch categories from pastime to, say, an entrepreneurial one over time.

Facebook is a classic example that illustrates this point. Mark Zuckerberg transitioned his "pastime" idea of connecting friends at Harvard one level at a time, until it became one of the most successful entrepreneurial showcases around today. So, as you can see, an idea can start in any category and progress toward the ultimate level of becoming a successful entrepreneurial business.

As I have said many times before, ideas are unlimited and opportunities are countless. What matters is whether you have FOUND your best idea. In which case, you now need to decide what you will do with it.

> *Ultimately, ideation is a blend of art and science: The art of generating creative ideas and the science of finding the right idea that you can convert into a reality.*

Given everything that you have learned so far in this book, will you know which is the right square into which to fit your final "winning" idea? Knowing that will be an effective way of grounding your idea, so you can then take necessary action. Ultimately, ideation is a blend of art and science: The art of generating creative ideas and the science of finding the right idea that you can convert into a reality.

What Venture Capitalists Want

One way of making your entrepreneurial dream a reality, of course, is to attract external funding. How do you impress an investor enough that they will want to back you and your idea? One way would be to insert

your idea into the relevant matrix box. This provides a useful visual that not only helps you to identify just where your idea fits, but also demonstrates to external investors or other interested parties that you have given a lot of thought to both the category into which your idea belongs, as well as the current market opportunity. By doing this, you are not wasting a venture capitalist's time by presenting them with a hobby or pastime idea that is not worth their investment.

Indeed, this is an appropriate point at which to briefly outline what VCs are typically looking for when entrepreneurs approach them with ideas. As part of the research for this book, we spoke with Ajay Goel, Managing Partner and Producer at Crestlight Venture Productions in Bangalore. Ajay is an unusual VC in the sense that his background includes corporate executive, businessman, entrepreneur, in addition to now leading this global, next-generation venture firm.

Investing in someone's idea is not an arbitrary exercise. As Ajay points out, it involves a lot of "science." As he told us, "We believe success can be engineered." That said, his firm rates early stage startups by scoring and ranking them according to their answers on 100 questions across five areas:

- **IP Protection**: How uniquely do you "own" this idea?
- **Leadership**: Is your team balanced, benefiting from technologists, someone skilled at sales and marketing, and a leader with deep business knowledge who can be the CEO? If there are gaps, the likelihood is that his firm will want to put in a temporary leader or mentor.
- **Global Ecosystem**: Do you already have global reach, with large corporate customers?
- **Storytelling**: Have you shown sufficient clarity of thought, such that you are capturing hearts as well as minds with your idea? Are you looking beyond marketing content in order to tell engaging stories to your market?
- **Exit Preparation**: Do you intend to become a large-scale enterprise yourself or align with a corporate player? You will need to determine

this at the outset so that, three years from now, you know in which direction you expect to be headed.

Unfair Advantage

One of the questions that Ajay asks himself as he meets with early-stage startup founders is: "Do they have an unfair advantage?" In other words, is this business uniquely qualified to succeed? Similarly, you will always be more attractive to those who may be willing to fund you when you have FOUND the problem for which you have discovered a compelling solution, you know your market inside out, and you have several early adopters that are willing to be your customers.

One of the most gratifying things we heard Ajay say when we interviewed him was that he makes judgments by "sitting on the other side." That is, he thinks from the perspective of a client or customer and whether or not the entrepreneur's idea and foundation for a business really meets *their* needs. By working your way diligently through the FOUND process, you will also be able to adopt such a perspective, because you will have spoken to so many people that you fully understand their needs and how your business idea can fulfill them.

Of course, all of this is somewhat moving beyond the intended scope of this book, which is focused on ideation. But it is nevertheless important that by now you should have a vision for where your idea can take you, especially if you intend to attract funding along the way.

Undoubtedly, you will still have a million questions popping into your mind. That is quite natural and normal. When I was originally discussing this process of ideation with my co-author, Dr. Liz Alexander, her curious nature and inquisitiveness triggered several additional questions that we both felt we wanted to address in a separate section. That is why, in the chapter that follows, you will find ten sets of questions and answers that may help to address some of the remaining queries you have.

Unlimited Ideas, Countless Opportunities

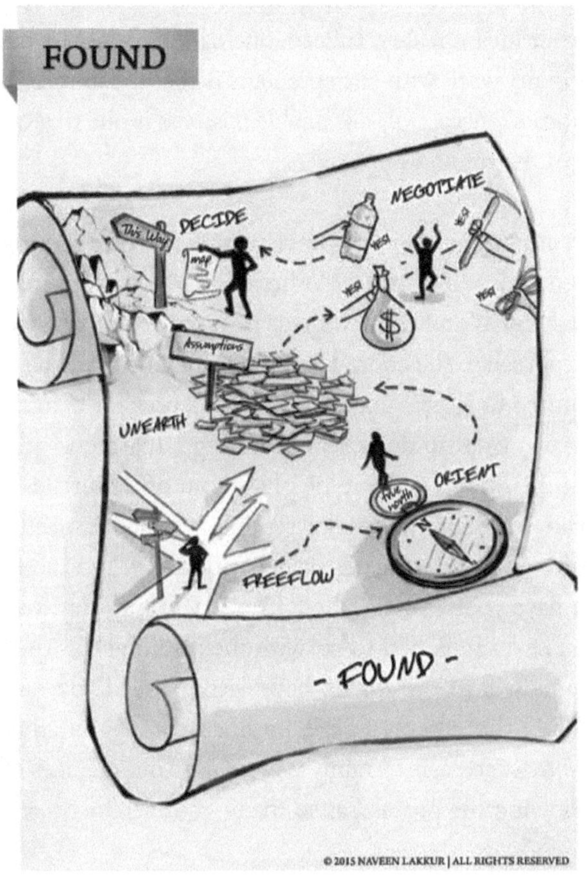

1. **Does the FOUND process need to be modified if I'm working with a partner (i.e., a co-founder), as opposed to setting up on my own?**
The FOUND process holds good regardless of whether you are ideating with one or more co-founders, or just by yourself. However, bear in mind that the same idea may resonate or orientate very differently with each one of you. As I pointed out in the Orientate chapter (Chapter Three), it is very important for your idea to be one that speaks to the life experience, values, and passion that you hold. This must be the case for each of your co-founders as well as yourself, even though the reasons each of you has for moving forward will be different. Please do consider this important point as it will help you to stay together in the journey of making your idea a reality. Indeed, one of the insights I have had over the years in my work with entrepreneurs is that the journey they embark on from idea to successful, sustainable business is one that completes the life story of the founder(s).

2. **What is your suggestion for those people who are feeling restless to get started and *do something?* Who are ready to jump into the entrepreneurial world and think all this process stuff is a waste of time?**
I always appreciate the energy and the restlessness one has, and indeed that's required to a great extent, in the entrepreneurial journey. But the last thing you want to do is begin running a marathon at the speed of a sprint. This is not a game to be played out of a spurt!

To make your experience a successful one, there is need for preparation. Shortcuts are short lived. Tactics will only get you so far. Indeed, if you don't have your strategy thought out, you may find yourself somewhere you never intended to be, with the resulting loss of time, money, and the goodwill of those who have accompanied you on the journey so far. While the process I have outlined throughout this book does not *guarantee* success, it certainly will reduce your chances of failure. It's worth following the process, as so many Founder Institute participants have done to their great satisfaction, as taking a disciplined approach at the outset will save you considerable time in the long run.

3. **I'm not sure there is an emotion underlying my business idea. It simply came from paying attention to online and offline conversations and realizing there was an opportunity to exploit them. Is that sufficient reason to pursue it, given what you say in Chapter Two?**

   If you go deeper and figure out from where and why the idea originated, you will surely find one or more emotions associated with it. In fact, now that you are aware of how many entrepreneurial ideas have been brought to fruition because of strong emotions, I think you will come to see that this holds true in the vast majority of cases.

   For example, when Liz was speaking with an entrepreneur in her home town of Austin, Texas recently, this man was recounting why he decided to move forward with his particular business idea and, quite unsolicited, said, "I was so angry, I could not have stopped myself doing this, even if I wanted to."

   However, bear in mind that when you are in the first, "free-flow" phase, it is not important to analyze where or why your idea originated. Just be as enthusiastic about generating as many ideas as possible and allow your creative juices to flow.

4. **In your experience, what's the most important thing that VCs look for when evaluating whether or not to fund an idea?**

   Great question! As Ajay Goel, mentioned earlier emphasizes, it is important to put yourself in the other person's shoes and to try and think in advance what it is they might be looking for from you.

   That said, there are many things that a VC would look for when they are considering whether or not to fund your idea. There is no single rule or framework that they tend to follow, which is why you might want to speak with other entrepreneurs who have already presented to VCs in the past, or read magazine or newspaper articles containing quotes that could yield valuable clues as to their interests and approach.

In the meantime, some of the points that VCs will want answers to, include:

- Is there a need for this idea in the market as it stands?
- Is there a big enough market?
- How unique is this solution?
- What do you know about the founder(s) and their relatedness/orientation towards the idea?
- What is your assessment of the existing team and it's ability to execute?

There could be many more such questions and certainly the points listed above are not in any particular order of priority. I would, however, add that at the idea stage, the commitment of the founder(s) to solve the problem with a fire in their belly—not least to grow and create wealth—is a paramount requirement to early stage or seed stage investors.

5. **One of the questions you posed in the Orientate chapter (see Chapter Three, page 33) asks if we would be prepared to live with our best idea for the rest of our lives. What about the importance of formulating an exit strategy? I'm thinking I'd like to build a business that will be bought out in 5-7 years. What's your advice on that?**

Certainly there is a need to formulate an exit strategy in most cases. There are two ways to look at this. On the one hand, it could mean exiting out the *investors* who trusted in the idea; on the other, it could be *you* that exits from the business. The concept of an exit strategy could also mean transitioning into a plan whereby the responsibilities of the founders has to change to support organizational growth.

Regardless of which of those two avenues is relevant to you, your approach should be to build a company that lasts; that stands the test of time. There should never be any doubt in your mind about that, regardless of how long you intend to be directly involved. You should stay committed to solving the problem, growing the company, and making the venture a meaningful and enduring one. While at the same time staying detached enough to be able to do the right thing for the business as it changes and grows.

Maybe you will get a good deal when 5-7 years is up. If it makes commercial and logical sense to do so, because your solution is more likely to grow quicker and more successfully in the hands of someone else, then you probably should sell the business. Then again, bear in mind that the new buyer may want to purchase your business only if the existing team commits to staying on to run it. In which case the biggest change is only in the share holding, not the original commitment, which still should be 100 per cent.

The bottom line of all of this? If you build on an idea that you really don't want to pursue over a long time period then it is highly likely that no one else will want to, either.

6. **Is it ever a good idea to hire someone else to conduct the research you're suggesting we do in the Unearth chapter? Why is it important (if it is), that we do this ourselves, given how time-consuming it appears to be?**

In some cases it might make sense to engage a professional company to do the market research, because they have access to resources that you don't. But it will still require your direct involvement in analyzing that research, ensuring that the data speaks to your values, and that you are emotionally engaged enough with the process and purpose of selecting an idea that can become a sustainable business.

"The devil is in the details," is an old but true saying. However, I also like to say that there are *gods* to be found in those details, too. While you might find it valuable to get some professional help or team assistance during the research phase, as the founder of your business it will make a huge difference if you are directly involved in finding

those little, all-important insights that will help secure your success over the long term. Aside from anything else, this will help you to build a plan on how to manage the "devils" when you encounter them, and engage with the "gods" so you can leverage them at the appropriate time. Remember, the Unearth stage is where you will find the gems and I think it behooves every founder of a business to be one of the prospectors that goes in search of that treasure.

7. **What should I do if I see a problem that my target market will likely face in the near future, but I can't convince these customers that it *is* a problem, since they're not facing it today?**

This kind of an idea fits into either the Greenfield or Unknown market stage shown on the matrix outlined in Chapter Seven (see page 75). While it is a great thing to have foresight, it also brings with it many frustrations when others don't see what you do.

Remember the saying attributed to Mahatma Gandhi: "First they ignore you, then they laugh at you, then they fight you, then you win." The same is true in the entrepreneurial realm with ideas that are outside the bounds of most people's imagination. (Which is why Henry Ford is alleged to have said, while in the process of creating his line of cars: "If I'd asked my customers what they wanted, they'd have said a faster horse.")

What all this means is that the length of the gestation period— that is, the time between people ignoring, laughing, fighting and then finally accepting your idea as useful to them—will determine your course of action. You are going to need to gauge how long it might be for the problem to be readily accepted by your market.

At this stage it could be important to peg the idea into the right category within the matrix. If we imagine the aforementioned gestation period to be more than 24 months, then your idea could be a potential candidate for patenting. But this should only be considered if the idea is new and novel, or if you have decided to move forward with it as a pastime project in the meantime.

Timing is everything in cases like these. Remember what we learned from Mr. Mani's experience with the Ask Me venture mentioned in Chapter Four (see page 43). Who knows, your pastime project could morph into an intrapreneurial or even an entrepreneurial venture eventually, in the same way that it did with Facebook.

If your idea is strong and the market is very large, and you have the right team to execute it, a long gestation period (say, anything more than 18 months), might make it a better intrapreneurial venture. In which case, you could look for a corporate sponsor that can help you develop the idea.

On the other hand, given the same basic principles—a strong idea, a large market and the right team to execute it—but with short or moderate gestation period (say, less than 12 to 18 months), it might become a successful entrepreneurial venture. *Provided* that you are ready to fund the idea with your own money initially. That is, until the market traction and adoption can be brought about.

8. **I'm not convinced it's a good strategy to share my idea with other people, because I'm worried someone will steal it and execute before I'm able to move forward. I'm really in the very early stages of developing my idea. What can you tell me to satisfy my fears?**
It is quite natural for everyone to believe that they have the next multi-billion dollar idea and I fully respect that feeling. But let's be practical here. Consider the following possible actions:

* If your idea is really new and novel, and if relevant, do a patent search; if your idea qualifies, apply for a patent. Study the procedures and take pride in owning the patent, as it will be a definite asset to you, albeit an intangible one. Alternatively, during this process you will discover that there are many more people who have had the same or a similar idea, even before you thought of it—but at least now you know that.

- The idea itself is only one side of the coin, the other is the execution. If you think it takes someone as unique and exceptional as you to execute this idea (for example, because of some specific life or business experience and knowledge that only you have), then you have got nothing to fear in discussing your idea with others. If, on the other hand, you believe that anyone could take your idea and run with it, then it may not qualify to be a "winning" entrepreneurial idea in the first place. After all, I have met a lot of very smart, capable people who had the idea of building a super search engine for the web, but it took Larry Page and Sergey Brin to execute the idea that created Google.

- If you are working on this idea as a pastime or hobby, then why would you fear it being stolen? Indeed, you have reason to *celebrate* if your idea is taken and developed into a business, as at least you know that the idea you created is worthy. And, after all, you would know for certain that if *you'd* had the wherewithal to do so— including the motivation, the business savvy, and resources—you *could* have built a business from it yourself. But you didn't!

Once again, never forget that ideas are a dime a dozen. Most people are too focused on their own ideas to worry about stealing someone else's! Focus instead on how you might go about building something out of your desire to solve a particular problem. Then cultivate the kind of positive, expansive attitude and courage that helps to generate unlimited ideas and the countless opportunities that will bring them to reality.

9. Most of the successful examples in your book seem to be about people, like Rajeev Pathak of eDream Edusoft, who want to change the world. I just want to find the best way to make some good money and to see if the entrepreneurial life suits me. Am I doomed to failure? Not necessarily. You might still get lucky, because in this case luck will play a major role. This is one quality that surely distinguishes gamblers and businesspeople. Both of these activities involve the element of risk. While one of them (gambling), is completely based on instincts with the only objective being winning (i.e. making money), the other (business), is focused on the journey of solving some problem in the market, getting paid for it, creating employment, sustaining something worthwhile, and scaling to help build the economy with the objective of creating broader wealth.

If making money is your only objective, then the entrepreneurial journey might be a painful one for you to bet on. In fact, taking a chance in a casino might be a better bet, although I don't recommend it unless you have money to burn. Instead, I would encourage you to embark on the entrepreneurial journey only after creating a meaningful context for yourself, in the same way that Thomas Edison went about building a legendary company like General Electric (GE).

If you study the life of any successful entrepreneur, you will realize that what they really had a passion for was not so much the business they built at the end of their journey, but the joy of seeing their idea become something successful and value-creating. For them, it's the journey and not the destination that is the real reward!

10. I've worked my way through your FOUND! process and believe I have what it takes for me to succeed. What comes next?

We can always continue to discuss the entrepreneurial journey and there is certainly sufficient additional material out there for you to read. But entrepreneurship is like swimming. In order to learn how to do it properly, and safely, you need to do more than just get your feet wet, you need to fully submerge yourself in the water. No amount of reading about different strokes and the correct form, without getting into the water, will help you learn to swim.

Therefore, I think it's important at this point to take considered action. Practice the process of ideation by generating as many ideas as you can. As you do so, check their orientation against your own life and values. Validate your assumptions about those ideas by finding those gems of insight. Talk to as many people as you can in order to crack the real deal early, and determine the future with solid evidence that backs you up. With a powerful context and the right intention, the world is yours to take.

❋ ❋ ❋

While we had originally planned for this to be the conclusion of the book, Dr. Liz and I have been inspired by so many additional entrepreneurial stories and successes that we wanted to capture at least some of them in these pages.

So, for the last part of our book in the following section entitled Been There, Done That! we offer six case studies of courageous entrepreneurs who either FOUND their winning ideas and transformed them into sustainable realities or are instrumental in enabling ideation in others.

Been There, Done That!

Six Stories of Ideation Experiences

The next few pages offer the experiences of six very different idea-tors. These stories will hopefully inspire you to move forward with your own entrepreneurial journey:

- **From Bricks & Mortar to Online Success** captures the experience of Dayal Nathan in dealing with the problem of too many ideas, to leveraging his skills, finding a co-founder and the initial market creation. As a bonus, he shares his ideation and startup wisdom to the aspiring entrepreneurs.
- **Prank to Path Breaking Growth** charts the journey that Srikanth Acharaya took to launch his first company, Gift Wrapped, as well as the trials and tribulations he has managed to overcome along the way.
- **Learning All the Way** shares Poornima Shenoy's journey of ideation and how she chose the industry and idea. Being a first generation entrepreneur, she talks about how a disciplined approach in the early days of developing an idea is now paying off for her.
- **The Journey from Ideas to Commercial Reality** is the inspiring story of Srinivas Varadarajan's shift from HP engineer to multiple award winning co-founder of Vigyanlabs, the creator of the Intelligent Power Management suite of products. Not least, how owning a considerable number of *patents* has boosted his company's standing in the marketplace.
- **Championing Ideation** outlines how Ravikiran Annaswamy went about developing an ideation course for students through the Center for Development of Advanced Computing (C-DAC) in Bangalore, India, and the importance of nurturing innovation in young people.
- Finally, **The Theory of Jackpot** offers "Venture Catalyst," Abdul G. Sait's rationale for why he invests in certain ventures and what he considers to be the most important factors for entrepreneurs to consider when embarking on this journey.

From Bricks & Mortar to Online Success

Dayal Nathan, Energyly

As an entrepreneur for the past 12 years, I've never suffered from any shortage of ideas that *could* be built into businesses. My biggest challenge was to kill off all but the most scalable and sustainable of those ideas. To find the one that survived rigorous research, as well as that intangible signpost for success: gut feel.

My background is in the bricks and mortar style of businesses, where you have an idea, get a project report, then go to the bank to sell your idea and for the bank's security you get a mortgage based on the fixed assets you possess. In that way the challenge of your idea, scalability and vision is limited to the security you can provide. However, I had also created an e-commerce site, along the lines of Blockbuster.com, that leveraged my 8 years' experience manufacturing movie and music DVDs. But when I weighed up how I might scale that option, I recognized that with Amazon coming into India I wouldn't be able to differentiate myself enough to compete, it would be too costly to go up against this major player.

Motivation and Emotion

Another idea that attracted me was to develop an online marketplace for service apartments. I even launched the beta version called roomtostay.com. After being advised to discuss this with five or six people who held no bias around the idea and could offer me invaluable feedback on its potential, three advisors suggested I move forward. But it seemed to me that by trying to compete with the likes of Airbnb and Booking.com I'd be entering an arena that was too big and already well established for a small, bootstrapped start-up to be successful. I've always considered it more important to be able to execute well on an idea that's doable, than hold to the dream of becoming the next Facebook or other "unicorn," and fall at the first hurdle. What propelled me forward was never wanting to say to my grandchildren that *had* I done this I *could* have been the Microsoft of India. Entrepreneurialism has never been about creating huge wealth or coming to the attention of the media for me. My satisfaction stems from knowing that I took an idea that resided in my head around solving some problem, and converted that into an executable business model that became a company with employees and happy customers.

My Personal Orientation

The decision to move forward with Energyly came from my previous knowledge, understanding and fascination around a particular market pain point. I knew, from my days working in manufacturing, how many factories and other bricks and mortar businesses were wasting huge sums of money every month on their power bills. This was the case earlier in my career when I was promoted to being head of a profit center, where I was responsible for all the expenditures and income of that department.

I realized we were paying USD $20,000 every month for the power bill in my department because our process of manufacturing required

24 hours of air conditioning and processed water. We conducted a small manual audit and after looking at the resulting analytics, realized we were using *five times* more power than we actually needed. After we installed smaller, more energy-efficient equipment, we were able to reduce that monthly power bill to USD $7,000. This story had been sitting in my mind for a long time, not least because I noticed how, as I came into contact with other businesses, the size and cost of their energy bills was something that bothered people. They just didn't know what to do about it.

When I came to Founder Institute I had to pitch an idea and wanted to offer something new. I decided that since energy was moving toward business analytics, in order to know exactly how much power was being used by every device to reduce costs and increase profitability, this would be the idea behind my new business. I knew the domain well because I'd worked for many years in manufacturing, and I was well aware of the pain point, including the fact that the existing solution—bringing in high cost Energy Auditors—was too expensive for most small and medium sized businesses (SMB). I believed that if I could develop a do-it-yourself device that was cheap and easy enough to use, that the SMB and home market would seize on that opportunity to reduce their energy costs significantly. That was how Energyly was born!

Addressing Assumptions

Perhaps our biggest "aha" around understanding what the SMB market was prepared to pay for our product came about when I went to meet with potential clients. What I realized was that the issue of energy bill consumption and cost is not top-of-mind for most business owners. What concerns them are things like paying their bills and their employees on time, finding money for taxes as well as delivering exceptional services and products. When something is not top of the client's agenda, the price point is critical. While we had an excellent proof-of-concept and had modified the existing third-party hardware so it was much easier to understand and apply, the cost of that hardware was still around USD

$2,000-$3,000. Very few SMBs were prepared to make that kind of investment, which meant we had to build low-cost hardware from scratch.

I cannot emphasize enough how important this issue of cost was for us in the Indian market. One of the most popular cars in India is the Maruti Suzuki and in one of the commercials you can watch on YouTube they use the phrase *Kithna dethi,* meaning "How much does it give?" or "What mileage are you getting?" This speaks directly to one major assumption we made: that by having great software and using reliable 3rd party hardware, people would be eager to buy from us.

> I cannot empha-size enough how important this issue of cost was for us in the Indian market.

My background is in plastics, not software engineering. I knew what I wanted, just not how it could be developed at a much lower cost. So I approached a local university whose students needed projects to work on and entered into a joint venture agreement with them. One year later, we were able to offer our clients the same exceptional level products, costing closer to USD $200-$300.

This price point fits within "suspense accounts." That's the amount of money—say, $200 up to $500 in larger companies—that a manager can access without needing approval from someone up the chain, since they are relatively small disbursements for purchases that haven't yet been concluded. By fitting our price point within that range, we were making it much easier for purchasers to take action without lengthy decision making.

The Power of Collaboration

One of the dreams I had as I began to envision a solution for SMBs and homes to reduce the cost of their energy bills, was to offer a mobile application in addition to our state-of-the-art hardware device. While conducting my research into whether such an app existed, I came across Dilip Rajendran, a software guy in Singapore who had developed something similar as a hobby, so that he could monitor the energy bill of his parents in India. After I wrote to him and we began discussing the opportunities, he came on board as co-founder of Energyly. Four versions later, we hit upon the app solution that was closest to my original dream.

Advice to Aspiring Entrepreneurs

To those aspiring entrepreneurs that think to themselves that they will work for a couple more years, make some money and then come back to their dream, my advice is: start now! I have known too many people get carried away by the security and regular income of a corporate job. They then develop a lifestyle that is hard to give up. Or maybe they meet their partner and then begin to have children, and their life takes a very different turn.

Even if you are a member of the younger generation, you should jump on your dream to become an entrepreneur as soon as possible. Your age is not an issue, to my mind. You may not have as much experience as someone who has been in the world of work for ten or fifteen years, but I don't think that gives people as much edge as it once did. As long as you understand the problem you are trying to solve and have researched the main pain points behind that problem, you have just as much chance of success as someone older.

I also have advice to offer people like me who come from a bricks and mortar background and are used to a lifestyle business. It's important to see things differently and not get bogged down worrying that you are not a tech geek or start feeling uncomfortable being among that crowd. I believe developing this kind of confidence was one of the greatest benefits to me of going through Founder Institute. When you begin to visualize the possibilities in terms of a bigger picture and can come up with products and business models and sales strategies where attracting finance, such as a loan or mortgage from a bank, is no longer a challenge, you discover that the only obstacles to your success are failing to take systematic action!

Dayal Nathan
Chennai, India

Prank to Path
Breaking Growth

Srikanth Acharaya, TouchStone Enterprises

On April Fool's day, 2005 I played a prank that changed my life. I was working for Infosys as a software engineer and decided to tell my friends that I had an idea and was planning to quit my job to start my own business. I had a reputation for playing pranks on people every year on April 1ˢᵗ, and all my close friends were wary of anything I said on that auspicious day. This year it had to be something so big that it would override their defenses against my prank. Back then, entrepreneurship was not a familiar word and Infosys was the Mecca for every engineering graduate. It was unthinkable that someone like me would quit such a fantastic job and start a business.

The prank caught on much better than I had expected. No one caught my lie. The responses were emphatic, ranging from "Are you nuts?" to "What's the plan?" Some seven or eight people had already asked me what business I was planning to start. To which, of course, I had no answer. Luckily for me, however, I'd been having a casual chat with a couple of friends the previous weekend about the T-shirt I received from my company. That led to a discussion about customized T-shirts being a good business idea. So,

when the last person asked me about my new company, I blurted out that I was starting a corporate gifting company!

Several questions followed that day about corporate gifting: what it was, how I would go about sourcing, what marketing I would need to do, and so on. As I answered those questions I began to define a rough business plan, and by the end of the day I had one in mind. Although I can't remember much of what happened when I told my friends it was all a joke, I distinctly remember thinking about my idea incessantly for a the next couple of days. I also brainstormed with my best friend, Srinath, who was then working for GE Lighting.

The Birth of Gift Wrapped

The more we thought of it, the more it seemed to make sense. All my friends were in different companies and they were getting all sorts of products as gifts, customized with their company logo. A little bit of research revealed that there were not many companies offering corporate gifts. In a matter of weeks, we decided to quit our jobs and start up. And thus our company, Gift Wrapped, was born.

Srinath came from a business family and it was clear that he was going to be a businessman, like most of his relatives. In some ways, it was a relatively easy decision for him to quit his corporate job. But I was from a middle class working family and every one of my relatives was either a banker, engineer or doctor. My dad was the exception, as he was self employed, and turned out to be the only person comfortable with my decision to quit. My mom, on the other hand, had nightmares and tried everything to make me rethink my decision.

Thinking back, there are a couple of triggers that influenced me to take the plunge. The first trigger was emotional. I have to give a lot of credit to Srinath. He was my best friend for six or seven years at that point and I admired him for his boldness, confidence and ambition. The vigour with which he was moving inspired me to stick to my decision, because I wanted the kind of lifestyle everyone in his family had.

The second trigger was logical. I was recruited into a leading software company directly from college and that gave me the confidence that I was intelligent enough to get another job, even if the business failed.

The third trigger was the opportunity. I thought to myself that nobody was really depending on my salary. I did not have a loan or kids that needed my income. This opportunity seemed interesting right then. Even if I got an opportunity much later in life to get into business, I was not sure if I would ever be as free to take the plunge.

> *Even if I got an opportunity much later in life to get into business, I was not sure if I would ever be as free to take the plunge.*

From Success to Success

Before I left Infosys, I ensured I introduced Srinath to HR and got Gift Wrapped empanelled as a vendor. To this day, Infosys continues to be a major client! One of our first orders came from Srinath's uncle, who was a distributor of fertilizers. Almost all of my friends—and my then-girl friend, now my wife—who were working for different software companies introduced me to their purchase managers, and we got orders from almost all of them. The reason I believe we were given those orders was the story that we had quit our software jobs to start our own business. We knew nothing about sourcing, customization, taxation, sales or logistics. Early on, we botched up in every possible way. But every time we would get away with it, because someone appreciated our spirit and it taught us a thing or two about the right way to do things. It was by trial and error and failing a lot that we learned everything there was to learn. It was amazing how much our clients, vendors, and even government officials would support us because of our tenacity.

Our start in business was really humble. A good friend allowed us to use his garage as an office. We used to look through the Yellow Pages for phone numbers and call from the coin booth to seek appointments. We would rush to potential clients who were willing to meet us, with samples of anything we could get our hands on. Once we got an order, we would convince the vendor to give us the goods on credit, we persuaded printers to print logos on the products, do the quality check, pack it and deliver it to us.

Call centers and business process outsourcing (BPO) were booming back then, and spent a decent amount of money on corporate gifts. The only problem was that they would all work at night and we had to meet clients at ghastly hours. After a while we realized that this was an advantage to us, however, as very few suppliers were willing to meet them at night. A lot of times, we would spend the day meeting clients and vendors, then meet BPO clients at night and return home during the early hours of the morning.

We love the corporate gifting business. Unlike retail, it was easy to enter, we did not have to invest in stock, and the margins were fantastic. Our income was directly proportionate to how hard we were willing to work. We worked hard, we hired, moved to an office, got a website, started a branch office in Hyderabad, it was all very exciting. We were not afraid of making mistakes, but we were quick to learn from them and run harder.

Boom and Bust!

In three years, we had grown to 15 employees and operated in two cities. Things were going great for us. Growth was phenomenal, clients were happy and we had a great team. We should have focused and continued down the same path, but then we made our most expensive mistake. We decided to diversify.

Laptop backpacks were a strong product line for us and we were receiving a lot of retail inquiries for them. We decided to start a retail store to sell backpacks. That was a different business from B2B and for the first time we started to bleed money. But that was not all. We were selling our bags through a few retailers and one of the malls wanted to know if we knew anyone who could manage a food court for them. We decided to get into that too. And before we knew it, we were in the restaurant business.

Now we had too many things on our plate and the problems were showing up everywhere. To add to our woes, September 2008 saw the

Lehmann Brothers crash and everyone was talking about recession. Gifts were the first thing to get cut and that meant we were left with liabilities and little income. Payments thinned down and we were in a phase we had never expected to be in.

We ended up consolidating, liquidated what we could, and got back to what we knew and loved most: corporate gifting. Things got slightly better over the next couple of years. A lot of our competitors were washed out by the recession and we were one of the few who survived. Again, we started to grow in terms of products, clients, and branches. By 2010, we were again exploring more innovative ways to scale up our business.

We created an e-commerce site and tried to sell corporate gifts through the website. That was a total failure, as no one was prepared to buy large quantities of products without first looking at samples. While trying different things, we created two services called LogoStore and Reward-Store. LogoStore was a online/offline store that would offer customized merchandise of a company to its employees. RewardStore was a rewards and recognition platform that companies could use for their long service awards, loyalty programs, and dealer incentives.

What Came Next

In early 2014, we conducted a series of surveys to evaluate how we could serve our clients better and to see if there were other markets we could tap into. There were a handful of opportunities that we identified. The top three were to sell uniforms, to export, and to sell stationery. We tested all three opportunities and all of them were found to be lucrative. But the uniforms and exports markets were already crowded, very competitive and not scalable, unless we were to set up our own factory.

A deeper look at stationery revealed that there was a huge void in the market. The industry was suffering with several issues like counterfeit products, unprofessional suppliers, inconsistent pricing, logistics hassles, and a lot more. Every office needed stationery and there was no quality player solving these business problems.

We knew about a company called Ravi Agencies, that was the leading wholesaler and distributor for stationery. We had transacted with them in the past and had a good rapport with the directors of the company. We were reintroduced to them and realized that both our companies were targeting similar clients, had complimentary skill sets, and a very similar set of values and ambitions. A few months down the line we merged and launched a B2B e-commerce/m-commerce platform called OffiNeeds.com. With this launch we tapped into a multi-billion dollar market that has hardly been explored.

> *We were reintroduced to them and realized that both our companies were targeting similar clients, had complimentary skill sets, and a very similar set of values and ambitions.*

OffiNeeds.com is the ultimate destination for businesses to purchase everything they need for their day-to-day operations. We believe in helping businesses become more efficient by simplifying these types of purchases. Our clients are small to medium businesses as well as a medium to large corporations. Everyday, we strive to make it easier and more efficient for customers to buy through OffiNeeds, and thus help them save time and money.

We want to be known as a company that is genuinely interested in helping businesses succeed. As an effort toward that end, I published a book entitled *9 Sure Fire Ways To Save Money On Your Day-To-Day Office Purchases.*

As I write this, OffiNeeds is being embraced by businesses of all sizes across India. We are on the verge of closing our first round of funding. And we believe we are on the path to being a leader in B2B e-commerce. In years to come, we aspire to be to businesses what Flipkart and Amazon are to consumers: the ultimate destination for all their office needs.

While new ideas continue to flow, what matters is what we do with them. We have learned to ask ourselves the question: "Can this new idea lead to path-breaking growth to our company?"

Srikanth Acharaya
Bangalore, India

Learning All the Way

Poornima Shenoy, Latitude Edutech

Teaching runs in my family, in which there are several teachers and Ph.Ds. My grandfather in fact was a high school math teacher. The business that I am in today—eLearning—is a modern form of teaching, albeit with the model of the IT Services industry.

I spent my early years as a professional working in the field of advertising and market research, after receiving a Masters in Business Administration. While I enjoyed that work, down the line the entrepreneurial bug bit me, with an increasing urge toward building a company of my own. So I ventured into the entrepreneurial world to build a services company, a head hunting firm that focused on the IT industry. My co-founder and I were young. We knew how to build a business but not necessarily an organization. We flourished, but with limited back up and next-line managers, we felt burned out after a decade. Nevertheless, the company grew to be number one in its segment by the year 2000, after which it was acquired by a venture firm.

> Since India-centric learning and training approaches were going to have a major influence and social impact, I chose the educational segment.

After a period back in the corporate sector, during which time I served as founding president of the India Semi Conductor Association, the startup bug bit me again. In 2011, I began exploring opportunities and found that in India there were two industry segments that were buzzing with business all the time: healthcare and educational institutions. Both had business models that were ready to be disrupted, sooner rather than later. Since India-centric learning and training approaches were going to have a major influence and social impact, I chose the educational segment. Not least, because online learning allowed me to leverage my prior experience, both with corporate and educational institutions.

I is For Institution

My past experience had enabled me to build a large network, so one of the first things I did was to identify formal and informal advisors as well as some core team members. Now, the 'I' would mean an institution, not merely an individual.

As a team we began generating ideas and narrowing down the possibilities. The educational segment was very broad. We flirted with vocational skills development, conducting management programs, enabling undergraduate programs such as engineering & medicine, as well as custom courses for the corporate world in the dynamic field of information technology.

As we were trying to figure out which area to focus on in the field of education, one thing became very clear. The purpose of my life has always been to empower people through education and to respond to the immense need in a young and growing country like India for the right kind of education. I wanted us to learn in new ways and have a broader impact. We started to learn more by digging deeper in each of the areas we listed and interesting insights began to surface.

In order to create the huge, national impact I wanted and build a scalable business, we knew we had to leverage technology as well as our experience and expertise. Content is king and that was going to be the way forward.

What We Learned

As we further studied the field, we learnt many invaluable things:

- While trends in education had changed, the courses being offered had changed very little.
- Good quality courses were available to a select few in the urban world, but not in rural India, where the need is just as great.
- Governments efforts were underway to enable the use of technology in rural India as well as urban areas, through the advent of "Digital India".
- The B2B e-learning segment was under-served in the market.
- Language, in particular translation into local languages, could be a barrier but also a great enabler in our country.

Now that we realized e-learning was the way to go, we attracted a number of subject matter experts into our network who would respond to on-demand engagements. Through our advisors we received some institutional connections that we were able to develop, that understood the market requirements and could help us augment those needs with the solution provided by our complementary skills. We soon became the preferred partner for institutions that wanted us to create content for their e-learning programs.

The Success of Latitude Edutech

Thus, I became the founder of the company we call Latitude Edutech. We successfully raised seed funding to build a customer-focused, online learning delivery model. I was determined from the beginning that we would be a process-driven organization and this stands us in good stead as we scale and grow. The new policies and movement created by the government to skill India and broaden digitization definitely created a momentum and an awareness. People started

> I was determined from the beginning that we would be a process-driven organization and this stands us in good stead as we scale and grow.

to see the difference of distance education to a quality driven, standards based online learning.

Most recently, we created learning content for an international specialty hospital chain that was aimed at bringing their practitioners up to speed on new techniques and customer preferences. This was not an easy segment, but we delivered to the customer's satisfaction on our very first attempt and I am really proud of my team for making that happen. This is the practical side of our business. How else can you reach busy people across geographies and across time zones synchronously and asynchronously without disturbing their work time and also maintaining consistency?

I believe that in the coming years e-learning will experience similar growth and models that the e-commerce industry has already been through. We've received a couple of offers to be acquired but I think the growth phase of this industry is still around the corner.

Most satisfying for me has been the opportunity not just to learn, but to continue to learn about content creation, business models, engagement models, revenue models and how each of these contribute to great teaching and learning experiences. Ultimately the business is about people, both the creators and the learners.

Poornima Shenoy
Bangalore, India

The Journey From Ideas to Commercial Reality

Srinivas Varadarajan, Vigyanlabs Innovations

In early 1996, Sri Vatsa, Franz Koppold and myself were working for Hewlett Packard, spending considerable time with the Amadeus team in Erding, Germany to understand their business requirements. The problem we were trying to solve was how to enable an application to connect seamlessly to the different airline reservation systems that used a wide variety of technologies systems across the globe. While what we were trying to do is easy today, at the time we were constrained by a server that was less powerful than most of the Smartphones currently in use.

Toward the end of March that year, after much discussion among the three of us, plus others within the HP team in Bangalore, we arrived at a possible solution. I spent a couple of days writing a short document defining the application program interface (API) and how this would work. We discussed it with our customers and they were delighted. During the course of the next year, we continued refining our approach and its functionality.

Our manager at the time, Ayee Goundan—a patent holder himself—put us in touch with HP's Intellectual Property Attorney in Singapore. None of us in the team or any of our other colleagues in Bangalore had any idea of filing a patent application, which took some six months to draft. We

ended up, in early 1998, filing multiple patent applications because of the number of innovations involved.

I found it a very enriching experience to understand the entire patent process, terminologies and jargon. Because of this experience and interest, Vatsa and I became patent coordinators, working closely with HP's attorneys, reviewing patent applications and mentoring inventors.

A Wealth Of Innovation

As part of the Architecture team I had the opportunity to work across various business verticals and their associated teams. We found many of those teams had innovated but failed to leverage that fact. During early 2001, we convinced HP management in India to hold a yearly technology innovation conference to showcase these innovations. During the first year we identified a wealth of innovative ideas and helped to file numerous patent applications, including those of our own software engineering process monitoring tool. This simplified and automated the way to manage software engineering processes, at the same time collecting and analyzing metrics. We continued to receive patents up to the time I left HP in 2005.

After a two-year stint at Dell, where we set up the Technology Innovation Centre and created various centers of excellence for technology and innovation, the entrepreneurial bug bit Vatsa and myself. After almost a month discussing what we would do and defining the vision, goals and objectives, we launched Vigyanlabs (*Vigyan* means science and technology in Sanskrit). Our vision and mission statements were: "To be a highly innovative science and technology company providing "clean and green" solutions, to enable our customers to create robust and affordable IT products and solutions."

While we offered technology consulting during the weekdays, the rest of the time was spent exploring a number of ideas and options. The first was an efficient and lightweight projector, but we were unable to source the right components. We also looked at converting a Maruti Suzuki 800 petrol car to a hybrid car, but couldn't get Maruti Suzuki to part with any of the drawings, or any mechanic willing to alter the car.

In May 2008, I moved to Mysore, talked to a couple of entrepreneurs at the Sri Jayachamarenjendra College of Engineering's Science & Technology Entrepreneurs Park (SJCE-STEP), and decided to setup an office in their Incubation Centre. In September 2008, we had a formal office at SJCE-STEP and hired a few engineers from the SJCE campus. From the confines of a busy Bangalore, it was a wonderful environment to work in, with clean and green surroundings.

Finding a Unique Value Proposition

While continuing to consult, we came up with some new ideas of our own, one of which offered a unique value proposition for scaling certain ticket reservation systems, without adding additional infrastructure. One that would work across Smartphones, PCs, servers and other computing devices. This came about because we really understood the market and had researched the needs extensively, including what patents already existed.

After our experience with earlier patents being granted almost seven years from the filing date, we didn't want to leave any stone unturned. We tried to make sure that our patent application was comprehensive enough for the patent office to quickly examine it. After working with a patent attorney, we filed with the United States Patent & Trademark Office in January 2010 and were thrilled to receive the first patent for Vigyanlabs in June 2012—a record two-year timeframe. Our extra efforts in writing a good patent application had paid off.

By mid-2010, in association with Ernst & Young, we got selected as the principal and application architects for India's national identity project, Aadhaar. The Aadhaar project was intended to provide a unique identity to every Indian resident, equivalent to the national identity or social security numbers present in other countries.

In June of that year, Mr. Shivakumar, the CEO at SJCE-STEP, and Mr. Rajaram Keelar the Program Manager encouraged us to apply for seed funding. We created a high-level business plan for creating the initial prototype of the product and were granted seed funding the following year (2011).

Developing Aadhaar

Aadhaar was an extremely challenging project, since there was no successful biometric system as large as the one that was required for India, and therefore no proven biometric algorithms for such a large scale project existed. We amassed a wonderful team of experts from around the globe and created the mathematical models for the infrastructure, computing, storage, network and power. During the initial pilot phase of the project, we faced a number of challenges in terms of the amount of power and heat that would be generated by the data center. When the technical specifications of the Request For Proposal (RFP) were developed, we placed a lot of emphasis on the high energy efficiency, more so than other vendors and better than even the most efficient data centers at that time.

> *The energy problems we faced while developing the Aadhaar project were, to us, further proof of the market opportunity to commercialize our patent.*

But after the Aadhaar project was over, we remained disappointed at not having found a good power management solution.

The energy problems we faced while developing the Aadhaar project were, to us, further proof of the market opportunity to commercialize our patent. Of the many ideas we had, we dropped most of them and decided to focus on power management. With some of the money we had saved during our consulting assignments, we hired a few more engineers in Mysore to help commercialize our power management patent. After a lot of research and discussions with our attorneys we coined the name Intelligent Power Management (IPMPlus/IPM+) for our suite of products.

By the end of 2012 we had an early beta version of the product and participated in the NASSCOM Product Conclave in Mumbai, where we were selected for the Enterprise Product of the Year Award. A year later, we received the NASSCOM Technology Innovation of the Year Award in Mumbai. And the awards kept coming. In September 2013 we were declared winners in the Cleantech category at the Red Herring ASIA event.

The Success of Vigyanlabs

After Vigyanlabs acquired its first U.S. enterprise customer—undoubtedly boosted by all the awards we had won—we got in touch with the Environmental Protection Agency (EPA) and worked closely with ComEd, one of the largest utility companies in the U.S. Since then, we have continued working with other energy utilities like PG&E, SDG&E, and Clearesult, all of which offer rebates for our Enterprise Personal Computer power management solution.

In April 2014, Gartner featured us in the Cool Vendors category for Green IT and we continued to win many awards, both as a "TOP 50" startup and an innovator in cleantech. After having our innovation featured in the Economic Times, India Today, Information Week, The Hindu, Product Nation and Inc Magazine, we started getting enquiries from many more enterprises. In order to scale our business operations, we raised additional capital from friends and family. With this additional capital, we established our sales and marketing operations in Mumbai and the United States. In December 2014, our former employer Hewlett Packard started bundling our product for the business PCs shipped to customers in Japan.

In January 2015, we are selected by the All India Management Association for the Dr. J.S. Junejo Award for Creativity and Innovation among Micro, Small and Medium Enterprises. It was a great honor to receive the award from Dr. Junejo himself. Around the same time we also won the Frost and Sullivan Award for Technology Leadership in Green IT.

Our drive for innovation has never stopped and we recently filed a few more patents for Peak Load/UPS Management and Sustainability dashboards.

At this moment in time, more then a million devices around the world use our product and, given the power savings, we have helped save more than 34 Giga Watts of power and made the world a little greener. As such, we have executed on our vision and mission statements to be a highly innovative science and technology company that provides "clean and green" solutions.

Finally, I would say that while having patented intellectual property (IP) provides startups with a valuable differentiator—uniquely positioning your product to give a competitive edge—being granted a patent doesn't necessarily lead to a commercial product.

Srinivas Varadarajan,
Mysore, India

Championing Ideation

Ravikiran Annaswamy, Inhabit Technologies

In 2004, I was working in Bangalore, India for a large multi-national organization with a strong Research & Development (R&D) center, a key element in the company strategy. There was intense competition within R&D centers across the globe on the selection of work to do for the future. One of the key parameters as far as our global CEO was concerned, was the impact each center made on the business through innovations and inventions. Interestingly, at that time, the Bangalore center had made no impact on IPR's (Intellectual Property Rights), or ideas for new products.

I led the innovation transformation program to help bring in an awareness of the need for innovation and its importance to the global business. However, it proved to be a daunting task to make these software engineers and managers understand the strategic importance of innovation, because their focus was on execution and quality excellence. We designed a 2-day ideation workshop series, in order to showcase some methods and techniques of creativity and ideation, which led to us producing a bucket list of ideas to work on.

> *It proved to be a daunting task to make these software engineers and managers understand the strategic importance of innovation, because their focus was on execution and quality excellence.*

This organizational transformation was a tough journey with several hurdles before innovation became an organizational habit. For a start, we needed to instill confidence in everyone that "no idea is a bad idea," and that everyone should come out with their creative thoughts without limiting themselves. We convinced our workshop audience of the benefit *to them* of innovation by reading some of the patents that had already been filed by our competitors. This created a "wow" feeling and helped to break down the myths surrounding creativity and innovation, since most of the ideas were simple. What these competitors had done was just to go through right process and articulate the key benefits.

Visibility, Recognition, Rewards

One aspect we often overlook especially in a corporate setting, but which is very important in this journey, is that of the visibility, recognition and rewards for every individual who has a bright idea. We ensured that our Innovation Initiative was given very high visibility at all management levels. But what worked best was to give the person who came up with a good idea complete visibility at global levels. The ideas were shown regularly at the global patent office and with global product managers.

The next stage was to provide "Ideators of the Month" awards, not just with a certificate but also by announcing the name of the top idea generating team to all employees. This generated very healthy competition and everyone now wanted to be an ideator. As a last phase, we added monetary awards to the mix, for ideators who filed IPRs or whose ideas were included in product roadmaps.

> Everyone can be an innovator, provided that the right support and recognition are available.

I had the privilege of being the "innovation champion" for the company for several years, with the satisfaction of seeing several patents and product ideas germinated and innovated from the Bangalore center, that received global recognition. This left me with the lasting impression that *everyone* can be an innovator, provided that the right support and recognition are available.

C-DAC Course

Ten years later, in 2015, I was in a conversation at Bangalore airport with the executive director of C-DAC (the Center for Development of Advanced Computing). We discussed the current state of startups in India and the importance of innovation. He raised the topic of how young students in their flagship diploma courses don't look at entrepreneurship as a career option and, more importantly, don't apply their ideas to creating something meaningful. We also figured out that these students have a two-month project window where the work is routine without any meaningful results. Excited by this potential opportunity, I explained what we had achieved in my previous company and asked for the chance to run an innovation and entrepreneurship module, called Ideanauts, for students that would be offered in parallel to their academics. Our goal was to come up with innovative solutions to real world problems.

I started the six-month course with an introductory ideation workshop in order to emphasize the importance of innovation to these students. It proved to be a hard pill for them to swallow as they wanted to complete their diplomas and find a job. This kind of project work was seen as incidental by them. Yet here I was, offering them an opportunity to make that project work interesting and challenging, so that they might have a new career option. Let's just say that there was huge resistance to the program, with the students not keen on participating.

The program was designed for regular interventions with motivational talks and a flow for ideation. With support from the academic team we were able to identify nearly 50 problems that could be solved and we fine-tuned that list to 30 of the most innovative ideas. It was a laborious process to convert problem statements into new ways to solve them, thereby unleashing the students' creative potential. Once we reached that stage of refinement, however, there was a natural excitement to move forward to a solution, with strong support from the top management.

An Emotional Journey

The entire process was challenging as most of the students wanted to apply technology without really understanding that what they *needed to think about* was how to solve a real-world problem. Our lengthy discussions with the students around orientation and negotiation, in order that they find the right applications, were experiences in themselves. Nevertheless, I enjoyed every part of the process to find the core of a problem and a solution for it.

At the end of the course the students made 30 demonstrations, which were a MVP (Minimum Viable Product) for the problems being solved. The emotions generated by the program, and the importance that the students subsequently gave to it even in such a short period, can be summarized by two incidents. In one, a group broke down in tears because they were not selected for final demo round. And in the other, a second team who made it to the final round broke down also because their demo did not work well. They had spent the whole night in order to get it working so that I could visit their lab the next day and see what they had built. This time it brought tears to *my* eyes, looking at the dedication and the passion for innovation our program had inspired in these young people.

> It brought tears to my eyes, looking at the dedication and the passion for innovation our program had inspired in these young people.

The majority of the ideas that came from this course have become part of the CDAC demo portfolio; a few of them are being set up as startups by the ideators. The program is now in its next phase and we are working on over 60 ideas, but we also expect to make a change in the way students learn and apply technology to real world problems.

On a personal note, this journey of helping young people embrace ideation and translate that to real world innovations has been exhilarating. I have coached individuals to be better innovators and helped organizations to transform ideas into innovative units. The critical success factors, as I see them, are to have open mind for ideas, to persevere, and to have the passion to take those ideas to a meaningful solution.

Ravikiran Annaswamy
Bangalore, India

The Theory of Jackpot

Abdul G. Sait, JGI Ventures

Life starts with a dream. Choice and chance play equal roles in helping you live your dreams. My journey started by chance. I was doing my Post Graduate degree when one day the education group chairman, Mr. Chenraj Roychand, announced that he would support anyone who wanted to become an entrepreneur. I didn't think much about it, but approached him the next day with a thought that I want to start a financial services company. You might ask, why financial services? That's because I was a passionate stock market trader from the age of 17. The day after saying this to Mr. Roychand, I received a cheque for INR 2.4 million, with no questions asked, and my journey as an entrepreneur had begun. Even now, I'm amused as to why Mr. Roychand gave me this money.

My first entrepreneurial venture was a financial services company known as Basket Option. But over a period of time Mr. Roychand shared with me his vision of creating and nurturing some 8,800 entrepreneurs. I was inspired to become part of this vision and thus began a new journey as a "Venture Catalyst."

The Life of a Venture Catalyst

As I write this, I have facilitated 24 ventures & supported 36 entrepreneurs from all walks of life. I am also strategically involved with 50 ventures within our parent body, JGI ventures. What do I look for when I invest in ideas? What did I see in these 24 companies, and why only these ones?

In a single year, I get to see an average of 150 to 200 ideas and then may invest in four or five ventures. What goes into that selection is a complex formula in my brain, which I had not thought consciously about until writing it down here.

Ideas are nobody's monopoly. There are millions of ideas, which are born every day and die every day. There are millions of people who get an idea every day and then forget them at the same speed. Out of millions of ideas and people, only a few succeed and very, very few make it big. I believe it's not because of the idea but because of the implementation of the idea, which is equally or more important than the idea itself.

> *Only a few succeed and very, very few make it big, not because of the idea but because of the implementation of the idea, which is equally or more important than the idea itself.*

I invest in people with ideas, not ideas with people. This means that the person, their personality, and their attitude toward their idea are more important to me. In particular, I look at how desperate the founder is toward their idea and how much they believe in it. Their hunger will determine the growth of their business. I look for the extent to which a person wants to bring their idea to life, and how far they will go to actually do that.

I also want to know what is the primary objective or values behind this idea? Is it only to make money? I'm not saying that money should *not* be a criteria. Of course, business has to generate money and make a profit, but the values of the founder will determine how much money the business will make—and in what way. If the idea is only to make money, then it's a short-term game as the business deliveries will undoubtedly someday become compromised. But if the idea is to build an organization, positively impact society, disrupt the world and add value, then it's a long-term game and will surely make a lot of money.

Don't "Build to Sell"

A recent trend among entrepreneurs is to "build to sell." I am not against this approach, but it is misleading. Only those companies that have a solid idea and the right execution capabilities will get acquired. Therefore, it should be every founder's priority to focus on building a strong, value-creating organization, not how or when they will sell that company down the line.

Another reason not to start a company solely with a view to selling it is that the culture and the strategies that fit around that may not be solid. Why do I say that? Because when we know we are *not* planning to do something for life, then our attitude toward it will be short-term and lacking in passion.

Let working on an idea and building an organization around that innovation be the *choice* and acquisition be the *chance*. This thought process is also the key to my selection process for investments. I am fine with making a quick return from an exit strategy, but strongly believe that without having made a proper choice that chance won't happen.

A great idea, of course, is the nucleus that holds everything together. It should be simple enough to explain easily to your market, potentially disruptive, or even just meet the need of the moment. It should have a good profit margin, because if the business doesn't make enough money it won't be able to fund its own innovative products and therefore cannot add value to the society at large. The solution should be competitive too.

Rebels Wanted

As a Venture Catalyst I am especially keen to understand the background of the individual founder. If an entrepreneur is a rebel, or has been a rebel, then they automatically get a brownie point from me. Rebels fascinate me, because they are people who dare to go in the opposite direction to everyone else, irrespective of the hardships. Maybe it's because I'm a rebel myself, given that I:

- Started a company without informing my dad, especially when he was busy setting up a factory for me.
- Gave up a lucrative family business to go in search of my identity.
- Became a pure vegetarian, which might seem a little odd with a name like mine.
- Started ventures and investing in people when the experts didn't approve of that.

For me it's a world of possibility, a world of faith, a world of conviction in which there is no place for negative people, those with a risk-averse personality, or that have no ambition.

> For me it's a world of possibility, a world of faith, a world of conviction in which there is no place for negative people, those with a risk-averse personality, or that have no ambition.

In the early years of my career as a stock market trader, I lost a lot of money. I paid a big price to learn my lessons. Which is why, four years ago I had an idea to offer stock market coaching classes, so I could share those lessons with others. I spoke to two men I knew who were from good families and were searching for a way to make their mark on the world; to execute on some idea in an important way. They shared the same passion I had for this idea and so we invested around five million INR in infrastructure and working capital. Since then our business has grown to become number one in the stock market coaching category within the financial education supermarket called Educesta. Although initially the idea was to run purely a stock market course, we also established the Stock Market Institute as one of Educesta's ventures. In the third quarter of 2015 we were close to earning a few million dollars for a minor equity dilution. I am happy that things are shaping the way we envisaged, but the business was never built to be sold. It was built to disrupt the education industry with innovative products, and leave the rest to chance.

"Passion Networking"

Finally, let me tell you about Karthik, someone who was my junior in college and who is a very active Rotary Club member. We knew each other well and I remember seriously mentioning to him that he should explore entrepreneurship at a young age. However, he later decided to join KPMG and build a professional career in addition to moving up the ranks in the Rotary Organization.

Karthik approached me recently with a plan to leave KPMG in the next two months. His idea was to help bring about a change in the way Indians choose their careers. He had observed that very few people were able to succeed in making their passion their profession. But he also saw that the day someone's passion became their profession, it was as if they no longer had to "work." We ideated on these thoughts and developed a "Passion Networking" platform.

In the meantime, I knew another crazy young man—Shubham—who had left his high paying job because of his aspiration to become an entrepreneur. His thirst for knowledge and hunger for doing something meaningful was fascinating to watch. When he expressed his ambition to become an entrepreneur, I suggested he connect Karthik to explore the possibilities of working together as co-founders.

Today, Shubham and Karthik are building a platform that will help those who are determined to live their passion. The business is known as Passion Connect.in and is one of the promising ventures that I am most passionate about. To date, the site has attracted 160,000 monthly visitors and is rated as one of the top 5,000 websites. It is currently in its beta stage and the real product is under construction. Once that is launched, I am confident the venture will create history.

My decision to invest or not to invest in others ideas depends on many things: their past experience, their beliefs, and their ideas. As long as an entrepreneur hits any of these, he or she has usually has cracked the deal.

FOUND

When you mix together someone's conviction, hunger and mental attitude with intuition and luck, you are bound to hit the jackpot!

Abdul G Sait
Bangalore, India

YOUR Journey Starts Now...

Finally, I hope someday that there will be an opportunity for us to meet. In the meantime, I would love to hear from you.

Please write to me at **Naveen@NaveenLakkur.com** outlining how you FOUND your winning business idea. I am always interested in learning more about how the FOUND process helped people like you on your entrepreneurial journey.

Good luck!

Contributors

Abdul G. Sait, JGI Ventures
Group CEO and Venture Catalyst

Abdul G Sait kick-started his first entrepreneurial initiative, a risk and wealth management company, Basket Option Pvt Ltd. during his 2nd year MBA in 2004. A serial entrepreneur ever since, he has over 20 successful ventures to his credit, each speeding toward category leadership positions.

A strategist with a hugely positive outlook, his strength lies in bringing together the best teams, along with ideation and mentoring aspiring entrepreneurs. With his "go-getter" drive he creates a contagious work ethos that is upbeat, bullish and goal driven.

Highly respected in industry circles for his innovative initiatives, business acumen and trailblazing success, Abdul prefers to attribute his achievements to his fundamental belief that "Success against all odds IS real success."

An outstanding orator, Abdul has been a distinguished speaker at the top business schools in India, inspiring all those he meets. Abdul is also an active member of networking forums like TIE, NHRD, BNI and prides himself in representing India as the Cultural Ambassador to Canada, as part of the Rotary Club's Cultural Exchange Program.

Ajay Goel, Crestlight Venture Productions LLC
Managing Partner

Ajay is an experienced and accomplished business leader, and hands-on technology savvy professional who has built and managed large technology solutions and services businesses for leading global corporations, including leading large transformation initiatives, business operations, strategy office, and system engineering teams.

He is a well recognized strategic thinker, with over two decades of experience. He brings along a sound understanding of high technology business and global relationships, having extensively worked in the cutting edge technologies space on cloud computing technologies, "internet of things," mobile platforms, big data, Information management & information security, smart grids, digital media, and industrial systems.

Ajay is the Managing Partner at Crestlight Venture Productions LLC, a global next generation venture firm offering "Lean Equity for Startups": a combination of early-stage funding with lean, accountable expert services for a disciplined and collaborative approach to building value and preparing startups for exceptional exits. Within the firm, Ajay is responsible for Business & Technology Strategy, Value Creation, and Asia Operations. He challenges the investment status quo by engineering the success of early-stage technology and innovative companies with a revolutionary system the firm calls "Venture Production."

He was managing director for Symantec Corporation for India and SAARC countries for many years. Prior to that he was Senior Vice President, leading the business, strategy and operations for Cisco Systems, India and SAARC. He also had a long stint with Sun Microsystems as the Country Director, India Business Operations. Ajay started his career with Asea Brown Boveri (ABB), and has extensive experience working in Europe, USA and in Asia Pacific geographies.

As an entrepreneur, he is a core team member of a successful high technology global start-up that built a cloud based universal interactive digital media delivery platform for high definition interactive content delivery across devices over the Internet.

Ajay is an active Rotarian, Paul Harris fellow, Louise Marchese fellow, Member of the American Chambers of Commerce, and a member of the CII National Committee on IT & ITeS. He sits on various boards of innovative technology start-ups globally. He is also a mentor at the Founder Institute and Stanford Ignite program, and is the past chairman of the Bangalore Round Table.

He is an engineering graduate in Electronics & Telecommunication engineering, and Stanford Business School alumnus.

Dayal Nathan, Energyly
Founder and CEO

Dayal Nathan, graduated in 1989 with a Post Graduate in Plastics Engineering with a Gold Medal from Central Institute of Plastics & Engineering & Technology (CIPET), Ahmedabad. He also graduated in Chemistry from Vivekananda College, University of Madras after completing his schooling at KVIIT Madras.

He began his career with VIP Industries, Nagpur as a Trainee Officer and later joined Nova Electro Magnetics, Chennai as Dy. Superintendent. He joined Pentamedia Graphics, Chennai in 1995 and had various assignments before quitting as General Manager (Compact Discs & Animation Business).

Dayal started his first company, Ojas Digital Technologies, in 2003, an animation studio that produced an animated feature film "Bala Pandavas." In 2005, he co-founded Solar Compact Disc, Chennai, South India's first DVD manufacturing facility and exited in 2014.

He has experience in many verticals including Plastics, Optical Discs, E-Commerce and Energy Management.

Dayal currently is the Founder and CEO of Energyly, an Energy Analytics Company that helps reduce power costs for business enterprises.

He has travelled widely to more than 20 countries and is currently based out of Chennai, Tamil Nadu.

Mukesh Jha, Autowale
CEO and Co-Founder

Mukesh is an engineering graduate from IIT Kanpur, where he focused on exploring every option available inside campus, from education, sports, music, and politics. He joined the chemical engineering stream but knew from his second year he wanted to work with computers. After spending a few years of his corporate career in Australia and Singapore with large multi-nationals in telecom and banking, Mukesh decided to explore more than just a comfortable weekday job and weekend parties. He wanted to work on problems within India to give people a better lifestyle by using technology, therefore chose Autowale, one of India's first rickshaw app company. Mukesh is a frequent speaker at entrepreneurship events in India and has been featured in the New York Times, Forbes and Fast Company for Autowale's innovation and impact in India.

Apart from his work with Autowale, he is still passionate about music and sings in karaoke parties with friends. Mukesh is married to Rashmi Jha, who is an MBA and worked with Citibank. They both love traveling to different continents.

Ivan J Goldberg, Vistage International (UK) Limited
Chairman

Ivan J Goldberg is Managing Director of Michael Adam Associates Limited, a management consultancy specializing in strategic planning. He facilitates the management of companies in the planning process and also acts as mentor to Chief Executives of many businesses. His consultancy was founded in 1982 and now has a long list of clients in a wide range of industries.

Besides running the consultancy, he also operates as a Chairman of Vistage International (UK) Limited with two CEO peer groups in the Manchester area.

He is a retired Chartered Engineer (CEng) and a retired Fellow of the Institution of Mechanical Engineers (FIMechE).

Harry Scrope
Brompton Bike Hire

Harry spent 8 years in the British Army serving in various theatres. Qualified as a chartered surveyor with CBRE Harry specialized in investment, planning and development in the UK and internationally. After 6 years in commercial property Harry became COO at Stonehaven, a leading boutique FTSE 250 executive search and international fund raiser. Harry joined Brompton full time in June 2013 to lead their Bike Hire business.

FOUND

Janardan Prasad, Autowale
Co-Founder and COO

Janardan is an entrepreneur who loves improving traffic conditions for living and improving his tennis skills for recreation. His passion for tennis and traffic both started in his college days at IIT Kanpur. Immediately after graduation he joined Media Labs, Asia and applied his creative skills to making animation films and computer games in order that education could become more interesting for rural kids without access to quality education. He is still trying to make things better for underprivileged kids in his free time, volunteering with an NGO (**www.vibha.org**).

During his IT career, Janardan worked in North America with financial clients, helping them build better payment solutions. His passion for traffic pulled him back to India where the traffic situation is getting worst day by day. Here he patented few of his ideas and entered into the world of entrepreneurship. A year later he co-founded www.autowale.in along with with college friend, Mukesh Jha. Autowale has been innovating by using existing infrastructure and resources to solve the big commute problem in urban India, for which the company was featured in national and International media, including the New York Times and Forbes. Janardan has also been listed by FastCompany as one of the Most Creative People in Business in 2015, for solving the rickshaw hailing problem in India.

Janardan is married to Dr. Shalini Saxena, PhD from IIT Delhi and PostDoc from MGH & Harvard Medical School, who is currently enjoying quality time with their 1 year old daughter Aarya.

Poornima Shenoy, Latitude Edutech
Founder and CEO

Poornima Shenoy is the Founder and CEO of Latitude Edutech. She has over two decades of experience as an entrepreneur and industry executive. Earlier she had been the founding President of the India Semiconductor Association (ISA) and was a member of its Executive Council for over six years. She has been actively involved in creating a brand for India in electronics and semiconductors on a global scale.

Poornima has been a successful entrepreneur and has seen her company's acquisition by an international venture fund. She worked with NASSCOM and the Manipal Group in a senior management capacity prior to ISA. She has been part of governmental committees and is an invited speaker at both national and international seminars. She believes that education and more importantly skills development of the work force can play an important role in driving the country's growth.

Poornima is a mentor at the National Entrepreneurship Network (NEN) and the Founder Institute. She is a government nominee to the Tripura Central University and an independent director on the Board of Moschip Technologies, a Bombay Stock Exchange-listed technology company.

She has been awarded the prestigious Chevening Scholarship for Women in Leadership & Management by the British Foreign and Commonwealth Office. She was co-founder of the group Women in Business and Technology (WBT) that later merged with eMERG.

She is an Economics graduate from Mount Carmel College, Bangalore and holds an MBA from TAPMI, Manipal. She has also undergone management development programs at the University of Michigan at Ann Arbor, USA and Bradford University in the UK.

Rajeev Pathak, funtoot
Co-Founder and CEO

Rajeev has a Master of Technology from BITS, Pilani and a management post-graduate from IIM, Bangalore. He has more than 20 years' experience in the technology industry, with the majority of his career dedicated to working with Wipro. He is credited with building a world class team of 1,000 plus people in Wipro, that delivered more than 20 products a year. He founded the Software Products Group there and boosted that business to US\$ 100 million within four years.

Rajeev has had some interesting milestones in the journey of building "funtoot":

- 2012 -Winner of Bloomberg UTV Pitch Contest where 1000 companies participated.
- 2012 - Finalist at a leading national innovation award where 400+ companies participated.
- 2011 - Filed patent for major breakthroughs in disruptive technologies in education
- 2011 - Launched "funtoot" an intelligent and adaptive personal tutor

Ramanathan N, 4R Recycling
CEO & Managing Director

Ram has handled a wide range of roles over the last two decades. Prior to co-founding 4R Recycling, he was Senior Vice President, Supply Chain at Tejas Networks, responsible for manufacturing operations. A key member of the senior management team at Tejas Networks, he had been associated with Tejas Networks since 2000 as part of its initial team. As

Head of Supply Chain he was responsible for sourcing, manufacturing and the delivery of Tejas Products by building a strong and efficient supply-chain organization, involving in-house sourcing, planning, program management, logistics and compliance teams. He also worked with electronics manufacturing services (EMS) companies to deliver cost-competitive products to Tejas customers. Prior to moving over to Supply Chain, he was Chief Financial Officer of Tejas Networks until 2007. Holding multiple roles since the inception of Tejas, he had contributed significantly to the phenomenal growth of the company.

His experience of over two decades includes handling Finance and Accounts, Operations, Infrastructure, Legal and Secretarial matters, Risk Management and Supply Chain. Prior to Tejas, he had worked in various organizations like Synopsys, Viewlogic Systems and Recon Ltd., in various managerial capacities.

Ram is also the Treasurer of the Hubli-based Deshpande Educational Trust and Deshpande Foundation, a sandbox creating an eco-system of innovators to address social challenges and sustainable social entrepreneurship in India.

He holds a Bachelors' Degree in Commerce and is a Chartered Accountant. When Ram isn't busy chalking out his big plans, he is busy listening to a variety of music.

Ravikiran Annaswamy, Innohabit Technologies
Founder and CEO

Ravikiran Annaswamy is Founder and CEO of Innohabit Technologies. He is working on various innovations enabling proximity marketing in the real world. As founder director of the Deccan Center of Innovation and Design (DCID), he works with young entrepreneurs, helping them to get started and achieve market success with a focus on impact

innovations. He was also co-founder and investor at Teritree Technologies, a personalized email marketing technology venture.

He has over 20 years' business experience as an entrepreneur and business leader at Nokia Siemens Networks and Siemens AG. He was business head for the Indian market, led Global Product Management and was the General Manager for Asia Pacific Solutions. He championed intrapreneurship by working as the innovation head for the Bangalore site of Nokia Siemens Networks.

Ravikiran has vast experience of launching successful technology solutions for global markets, mainly in the area of analytics and marketing automation, online billing and charging, innovative 3G/4G applications, multimedia and security solutions.

He is also engaged as a professional volunteer, currently the Chairman for IEEE Bangalore section and Industry Relations for IEEE, Asia Pacific. He is considered to be a thought leader and speaker at various prestigious international business conferences. His work has been recognized by several awards: Siemens Director's award for Innovation; Customer management and Project Execution, IEEE Bangalore: Best Volunteer award; runner up at AIMA's National Contest for Young Managers; and Asia finalist at Global Social Venture Competition conducted by UC Berkley's Haas School of Business.

Ravikiran's specialities are entrepreneurship, impact innovations, strategy formulation and execution, sales and business development, product management, service delivery, product engineering and technical support.

His MBA is from the Indian Institute of Management (IIM), Bangalore and he has graduated from UVCE Bangalore.

Srinivas Varadarajan, Vigyanlabs Innovations
Co-founder and CEO

 Srinivas is an innovator, entrepreneur and has assisted businesses in solving complex problems by building products and solutions that meet and exceed customer expectations. His innovations are in the areas of Intelligent Power Management (**http://www.ipmplus.com**), performance engineering and networking.

He has a Masters degree in computer science from IIT Bombay and over 24+ years of experience in the IT industry.

He is currently the founder and CEO for VIGYANLABS a startup engaged in innovation, technology andcConsulting. He also served as a Principal Architect for the Aadhaar program of UIDAI.

Prior to that he worked as a chief architect at Perot Systems, Bangalore where he was responsible for technology strategy, managing the technology centres of excellence.

His interests and specialties include energy management, sustainability, green IT, data centre design, innovation, technology strategy, enterprise architecture, SaaS, software engineering, performance engineering, knowledge management, networking & rich media. During his 10+ year stint in HP he architected many large complex solutions in Airline, Logistics and Financial Services. He was also a part of the Architects team for many of HP's middleware products like HP e-speak, HP ORB, HP Application Server, HP Content Distribution Server. At HP he obtained two patents in the area of design of high performance multi-protocol communication stacks. During his stay at Hughes, he lead the team, designing and implementing multi-protocol routers and bridges.

Subsequent to his Masters degree at IIT Bombay, he spent an year at IITB as a project engineer where he developed popular open source products (YAPCBR- Yet another PC Bridge) and IPXWatch (an IPX Protocol Analyzer).

Srinivas speaks often at various industry/academic forums and events. He is a mentor at Founder Institute and his other interests include astronomy, Ayurveda and alternative medicine.

Srikanth Acharaya, TouchStone Enterprises
Co-founder and CEO

Srikanth Acharaya started his first business when he was 12 years old. Wrestling was a favourite sport among kids back then and he had fallen in love with "trump cards". Everybody in his apartment and school was fascinated by his set of WWF trump cards that he had "customized" himself. He started procuring stamp size pictures of the wrestlers and made posters and cards from them which he sold to his friends. He believes this was his first experience of entrepreneurship.

Srikanth is a very passionate entrepreneur who co-founded a B2B e-commerce platform called OffiNeeds.com. He aspires to build India's top office supplies company. Through their cloud based e-commerce platform, the company makes it very easy and effective for business owners and corporates to plan and purchase all their office supplies requirements. Their product lines cover stationery, IT consumables, corporate gifts and housekeeping materials.

Srikanth specialises in procurement, operations, sales, marketing, building teams, and motivational speaking. Srikanth is also a mentor for entrepreneurship, an ardent traveler and foodie. He has published a book titled "9 Sure Fire Ways to Save Money on Your Day-to-Day Office Purchases."